FISHERS OF MEN

A LEGACY OF DISCIPLESHIP

NITA BRAINARD

2024

Harvey, North Dakota

ISBN: 9798325863493

Cover art by basikstudios, Omaha, Nebraska

Scripture quotations are from the King James Version unless otherwise noted.

Other versions used: New King James Version®. Copyright © 1982 by Thomas Nelson. Used by permission. All rights reserved.

New International Version, NIV. Copyright 1973, 1978, 1984, 2011 by Biblica, Inc.

English Standard Version® (ESV®)
© 2001 by Crossway, a publishing ministry of Good News Publishers.

Amplified® Bible (AMPC), Copyright © 1954, 1958, 1962, 1964, 1965, 1987 by The Lockman Foundation
Used by permission. lockman.org

Dedicated by Phil and Tammy Kleymann
to the memory of Louise Hamilton,
our spiritual mentor and fishing instructor

Table of Contents

Driving Away 1
    Divorce 1
    Mary 2
    Marriage 3
    Omaha 4

Cinderella 6
    The Farm 7
    Home Life 9
    The Hospital 11
    Loneliness 12
    Additional Abuse 14
    The Big Night 15

A Rude Awakening 17
    Culture Shock 18
    Little Sister 19
    Church 22
    Sickness 23

A Place to Call Home 25
    Home 27
    Joe 28
    Cowboys 30

Grandma 31
    Bill Fear 33
    Young People Upstairs 35

The Hairs of Her Head 36
    The Study 39
    Desires of the Heart 40

God or Me 42
- The Comet 43
- The Fight 44
- A Light in the Window 45
- It's Real 47

Mick 49
- Teenage Alcoholic 50
- Death to Sin 51
- Wanderer 52

Kim 54
- A Refuge 57
- Not Alone 58
- Covid 60

Relationships Redeemed 62
- Wedding 63
- Muskies 64
- Betty 65
- Mary and Ivan 66

Resolution 69
- Healing 70
- Mercy 73
- Need of Grace 73
- Channing 74
- Scars 76

New Life 78
- Public Testimony 79
- Kelly Kleymann 80
- Tim Kleymann 81
- Grandma's Influence 83
- Soaps 86
- God's Provision 86
- Etchings 89
- Jonathan Channing 92
- Grandma's Passing 94

The Spirit at Work 96
    Smiley 97
    Racecar Driver 97
    Aztec Mike 98
    Youth Group 100
    Demons 102

Chalk Talks and Camp Work 105
    Chip 106
    Golden Image 108
    Mila 109
    Ryan 110
    Justin 111

Page Turners 114
    Scripture 115

Testimonies 119
    Renee Groene 120
    Erin Strawn 121
    Daniel Ginn 122
    Shane Snipes 124
    Jerrad Wesack 126
    Brett Henn 129
    Eric Benson 130
    Mike Matulka 134

Josh 138
    Public School 140
    Wyoming 142
    Answered Prayer 143
    Starting Over 145
    Joanna 147
    North Dakota 148
    2020 149
    Israel 150

The Choice to Serve 152
    A Fishing Hole 152

Earthly Kingdom	153
Tim Yokom	155
Motorhome	156
Bible Study	158

Tim Van Hal 160
False Conversion	161
Conviction of Sin	162
True Faith	165

Eternal Hope 167
Randy Hoefs	168
Jail Ministry	169
Eternity	171

Love, Joy, Peace 173
Love	173
Joy	175
Peace	175

Scripture Index 177

CHAPTER 1

Driving Away

"Don't leave," the beautiful, dark-haired woman screamed. Her arm plunged through the open window of the station wagon. She grabbed the driver's hair and yanked it out of his head as he backed the car out of the driveway. Wild with anger and wrenching pain, she continued to scream as he pulled away. "Don't take them away from me!" To no avail. The car drove down the street, and they were gone.

Tammy never saw her parents together again. This painful memory, from when she was five years old, is her only recollection of her mom and dad in the same place. She and her older brother, Mick, and baby Kim were in the car with their dad. He took them to a trailer house in a mobile home park near his veterinary clinic in Omaha, Nebraska.

Divorce

In 1965 it was unusual in divorce cases for fathers to get custody of their children. Channing Cotton had readily convinced the court that he was a more reliable parent than his wife. Mary was mentally ill. She had experienced extreme mood swings all her life and had allowed them to control her. Her behavior was unpredictable and irresponsible. Besides that, she was notoriously unfaithful and had run Channing deeply into debt.

Mary was so absorbed with herself that she lacked motherly instincts. She didn't care properly for her babies. She didn't hold them or change their diapers. Channing came home from work to find his children badly in need of basic care, including removing heavily-loaded diapers.

Mick, at around eleven years old, was the oldest child. Two daughters had been born after him. Both had died. Due to their mother's character, the deaths were clouded in suspicion. Cheryl Anne died of a blood disease while in the hospital after her birth. Mary was not charged with any wrongdoing, but poisoning was not out of the question. Later, Sandra Marie died at a few months old, reportedly of SIDS.

The surviving children suffered various mishaps and unexplained injuries. Mick had a broken leg. Tammy had been thrown down the stairs. Worse, Tammy's mother had tried to sell her to a family acquaintance. With these reports and more, it was no surprise that Channing got full custody of his three children.

Mary

Tammy's mother had fiery, Irish heritage. She had been given the name *Kelly Ryan* at birth. Her name was changed to Mary Frances when she was adopted by a childless couple in Mitchell, South Dakota. She was a pretty girl, with a beautiful head of thick, black hair.

When Mary was still an infant, she had had four different illnesses at one time. Her parents expected her to die, and they had last rites performed by an Episcopal priest. Mary lived, however, and her parents spoiled her rotten. She never learned to control her passions or to appreciate the love that her adoptive parents showered on her. At the age of fifteen, she attacked and beat up her mother.

Driving Away

Mary got a new wardrobe every school year. By showing it off, she alienated the other girls in her small, midwestern town. She concentrated her efforts on gaining the attention of the boys, which was readily obtained. While she was still a teenager, she became pregnant. Her parents sent her to California where she gave birth and put her child up for adoption. Mary returned to South Dakota.

Marriage

Channing Cotton was the son of a South Dakota businessman. He had been sent to work on a dairy farm when only eight or nine years old. Treated roughly by his father, Channing pushed himself to success. He attended the School of Animal Science at Iowa State and excelled.

The aspiring veterinarian was overwhelmed by Mary's stunning beauty, and he determined to marry her. His parents, aware of her loose character, were staunchly opposed to the idea. They refused to attend the wedding, but he went through with his plan in blind defiance of their warnings. Channing and Mary were married in the early nineteen fifties.

Large animal veterinary work required long hours for Channing and put stress on his family life. He was always on call, especially during calving season. Disgruntled over his unpredictable schedule, Mary engaged in various ploys to try to win her husband's sympathy and attention. Her efforts led to unreasonable, and almost unbelievable, extremes. While the couple were out hunting together, Mary intentionally shot herself in the foot. The incident failed to give Mary the results she had hoped for. Channing threw himself the more into his work. While he was busy, Mary sought and won the attention of the immoral men of the community.

The wound in Mary's foot developed gangrene, and her leg had to be amputated below the knee. With the help of an artificial leg extension, she was able to walk normally, having only the slightest limp.

Omaha

After completing his residency, Channing bought a small animal practice in Omaha, Nebraska. Did he think it would benefit his family life to get away from the wagging tongues of the small town? The townspeople knew the promiscuous behavior of his wife all too well. She had thrown herself at every willing participant to her sin, and she had found plenty of takers. There would be more in Omaha, but perhaps her unfaithfulness would be less noticeable in the city.

Whatever Channing may have thought about his wife and family when he first moved to Omaha, his sights soon turned elsewhere. He hired a beautiful nurse to be his assistant. Betty had her own marriage problems, and she was ready for a change. In Channing, she found her opportunity. Her charms quickly overwhelmed whatever feelings Channing may have maintained for his wife. He divorced Mary and moved with his children into a trailer home near his practice. When the divorces were finalized, he and Betty married. Channing then moved his family to her house at 502 N. 74th St., Omaha, Nebraska.

The interim spent in the mobile home park was unremarkable, providing only blurry memories. Tammy's little sister was too young to play, but Tammy and Mick scampered around the trailer park. One time Mick convinced Tammy to cross the creek on a sewage pipe. The two children played in the woods on the other side. While they were there, it started to sleet. The sewage pipe was getting slippery. Mick crossed over and urged Tammy to follow. She started across but slipped. Frozen with fear, she looked down to what seemed certain death if she let go of the pipe. She clung for dear life while Mick ran to get his dad. Channing left his office and came running, but he didn't dare get on the pipe himself. It was too slippery and too risky to try to carry the frightened five-year-old across. He was about to go inside to call the fire department when he found a large branch. He held it out for Tammy to hold onto. Finding the confidence to switch her grasp from the pipe to the branch, she grabbed it, and her dad pulled her along the slippery pipe until she was safe on hard ground.

    Years later, Tammy had a similar experience in the spiritual realm. Following the example of those around her, she found herself in a dangerous position. She slipped on the icy supports that the world has to offer, and she saw herself as hanging over a dangerous precipice. There was nothing she could do to save herself, but she reached out and laid hold of the salvation that was offered to her. She trusted in the goodness of the one who held out the branch and allowed him to pull her into fellowship with himself.

For by grace are ye saved through faith; and that not of yourselves: it is the gift of God: Not of works, lest any man should boast.
—Ephesians 2:8-9

CHAPTER 2

Cinderella

When Channing Cotton divorced his beautiful but selfish and manipulative wife, he did not learn his lesson. His new wife was outwardly gorgeous and inwardly just as wretched as the first. Betty may have been more faithful to her husband than Mary had been, but she was not committed to his family. Her jealousy for his time and attention took a different form of manipulation. She was, unfortunately, more successful. Her control over Channing caused him to turn against the precious children whom God had entrusted to his care.

Betty had two teenage daughters. The three of them treated six-year-old Tammy with the disdain of the wicked stepmother and stepsisters toward Cinderella. Tammy was blamed for every mishap in the home, whether real or contrived. Like Cinderella, she was confined to her room and banished from most family interactions. Her meals were brought to her room. The dining room, as well as the rest of the house, was off limits. The kitchen was reserved for interrogation and beatings. The bathroom was accessed only for Saturday baths. For everyday use, there was a soup pot under the bed.

Betty and the girls cuddled and loved on Kim while she was a baby. Tammy, however, was viewed as a nuisance at best.

Their brother, Mick, stayed in the house only about a year. As soon as he was old enough, he chose to live with his mom.

Self-preservation and survival were Tammy's main goals. She was a compliant child, never intentionally rebellious. She had already learned to stay out of the way and avoid trouble as much as possible. What a devastating and confusing surprise when she was called to the kitchen at Betty's house! Betty pointed to a gouge in the furniture and demanded to know why Tammy had done it. She then stood to the side while Channing beat his daughter until she admitted to the crime. Once she confessed, Tammy was beaten even more severely, then sent to bed. This scene repeated over and over as the days dragged into months and the months into years in Tammy's new *home*.

The Farm

Around the time that Tammy was entering the first grade, Betty's older daughter was planning a wedding. Betty didn't want Tammy around to spoil the festivities, so Channing arranged for her to spend the upcoming school year with his sister Cheryl on a farm near Canova, South Dakota.

Cheryl was told that Tammy was naughty. She naturally believed her brother's report and expected the worst. The only real trouble that she had with Tammy, however, was that her little niece couldn't control her bowels after drinking orange juice.

Tammy had been baptized in a protestant church. Cheryl and her husband were Catholic, and they sent their children to a Catholic school. Tammy went with them and attended daily mass. As a Methodist, she was not allowed to partake of the elements, so she sat in the pew while the others went forward to receive the sacrament. Mass came after breakfast, and her bowels were difficult to control while she sat in the pew. There were quite a few accidents before the link to orange juice was discovered.

Tammy was a child with her childish faults, but she was no different than her cousins, and no naughtier. When she threw something at her cousin and wounded him, she justly deserved the spanking she received for it. She felt her guilt and didn't object to her punishment.

Cheryl's husband Rusty thought something was amiss regarding Tammy and her family situation. He told Cheryl that things didn't seem quite right. When Cheryl later learned the truth about how Tammy was being treated at home, she felt terrible for having never asked how things were. On Tammy's part, she didn't even think of telling anyone about the abuse at home. It was her world, and she kept it to herself. While at her aunt's farm, she was glad to be away from it. She thoroughly enjoyed the year with her aunt and uncle. She felt safe with them, and she loved being outdoors. She made mud pies, ran in the fields, and rode the pony with her cousins.

The farm didn't have the luxuries of Betty's city home. There was no bathroom. The toilet was an outhouse, and weekly baths were taken in a tub. Cheryl used a hand pump to fill the kitchen sink. Tammy slept in a little closet at the top of the stairs. But she felt loved, and her year in South Dakota was by far the best of her childhood.

Tammy was intrigued by what she witnessed at the Catholic Church. She knew that the answers to life's difficult questions would be found in religion, and specifically in the Bible. She saw the old women gather at the church with their heads covered. They mouthed words so intently, and she wondered who they were talking to. They looked so holy. She wished she knew the God they appeared to be communing with. She heard a little about Him in Sunday School. "Who are you?" she wondered. "If you are God, help me."

The months in South Dakota came too quickly to an end. Once a year, Channing took his family to a resort in Minnesota. He went musky fishing, and the family enjoyed a vacation. On his way from Omaha to Minnesota, Channing usually stopped to visit family in South Dakota. He picked Tammy up on his way north, and she resumed life with him and Betty.

Home Life

No damage to furniture ever occurred at the resort, and there were never any beatings while the family was there. Back in Omaha, however, after the vacation at the lake, the physical abuse started again. Kim was sharing in it now. The two girls had a room together where they spent almost all their time. It was well-stocked with toys, including a kitchen set, dolls, and games. Tammy and Kim played together every day, and they never fought. Tammy was forbidden to play Mommy or do or say anything that might let on to Kim that Betty wasn't Kim's birth mother. She obeyed.

Tammy and Kim were too young to understand or express the swirl of conflicting emotions they felt. They never talked about their lot in life. They knew there was no way out. No temper tantrum, no expression of frustration or heart-felt plea was likely to help their situation. Those things are for children who instinctively know that their parents love them. Betty did not.

Tammy believed that her dad loved her, but not enough to stand against Betty. Though strong in business and successful in the eyes of the world, he was too weak to defend his vulnerable children from his wicked wife. So completely manipulated was he, that he went along with the fabrication that his daughters were unreasonably naughty. Without witnessing the supposed deeds himself, he punished the girls unmercifully, using his fraternity paddle from Iowa State. Betty was always near, overseeing the process, but it was Channing's hands that swung the paddle. That paddle, which was an item of pride to her father, became a symbol to Tammy of the horror of her childhood.

When Channing died, he must have forgotten how it had been used. He left it to Tammy in his will. She burned it.

About three nights a week, sometimes more, sometimes less, when Dad got home from work, Betty would show him the pitiful evidence of his daughters' supposed naughtiness. It might be as early as 6:30, but often it was much later. Sometimes the girls were awakened from their sleep to face the consequences of their alleged deeds. The evidence might be a scratch in the wooden furniture or a cut in the upholstery. Both girls would be called to the kitchen. They stood with their backs to their dad and their hands on the kitchen counter. Dad would paddle one and then the other, back and forth until one confessed to the crime. The innocent party would be released to go to the bedroom. The one who confessed would be beaten severely as punishment for the deed.

During her punishment, Tammy was required to give a reason for her misdeeds. Of course every "reason" was a lie, because she had never done any of the crimes she was accused of. She and Kim were barely out of their room. They didn't dare leave. They were not locked in, but they were sent to their room whenever they were home, and their stepmother carefully placed a strip of white surgical tape across the doorframe. Frequently, this tape was mysteriously broken and added to the manufactured evidence of their supposed misdeeds.

Sometimes Tammy would hear hushed voices outside her bedroom door. She knew Betty was there, and she had removed the flimsy white tape. She knew accusations of vandalism and a severe beating awaited her. Dread over the upcoming beating would haunt Tammy all day. The punishment would come whenever her dad got home from work. Concentration for school was out of the question. On top of the ongoing physical pain from previous beatings, Tammy was frequently plagued by the torture of impending doom. She barely paid enough attention to pass from one grade to the next.

As Tammy got older, resentment for the abuse she endured built up more and more. While she was being beaten, she fantasized about opening the nearby kitchen drawer, pulling out a knife, and killing both Betty and her father. She never attempted it.

The girls took turns confessing to the made-up crimes. When the one who took the punishment crawled into bed, the other would comfort her the best she could. They never talked about it. They just loved and hugged each other.

Dad came into their room at night, emptied the pan that they kept under the bed in lieu of a toilet, kissed them on the forehead, and told them he loved them. This one act of love was a glimmer of light in their very dark world.

The Hospital

Tammy got to visit her mother for short periods every now and again. One time when she had come home from her mom's, she thought of a new *reason* for the erratic behavior she was accused of. She had already used all the common explanations, "I felt like it," "I was mad at Betty," etc. She had run out of excuses. This time she said, "I heard voices that told me to do it." It was a lie, just like all the other reasons, but it got her committed to a mental institution.

Tammy enjoyed her stay at St. Joseph's Hospital. It was peaceful there. She went to a concert, visited with the other patients, and started drinking coffee. She missed her sister, of course, but she wasn't being beaten. And she had more freedom than she was used to. The doors going outside were locked, but she could roam the halls.

Tammy attended group therapy sessions with people of varying ages. She didn't speak much during the sessions, at least not about anything pertinent to her situation. Certainly, she said nothing about the real reason she was there.

Ten-year-old Tammy determined that if she ever got a chance to speak with a counselor alone, she would talk about the abuse she experienced at home. The opportunity never came. She had personal counseling sessions once weekly on Thursdays, but her stepmother was always present. In Tammy's young mind, it really didn't matter that much. Who would believe her anyway? Her dad was a well-known and highly respected veterinarian. Her parents moved in the highest social circles in Omaha. The wealthiest and most influential people of the city sought out her father to trim their dogs' ears. These people would never believe his daughter was being abused.

Besides therapy, Tammy had other procedures done. At the time, she had no idea what they were. She lay on a table while metal pieces were attached to her head. She endured this treatment numerous times during her stay at the hospital, which may have covered a full school year. Only much later did she learn about Electroconvulsive Therapy. The shock treatments were probably designed to cause her to forget her mother. They did not accomplish this end, but they may have had a positive effect by dulling or obscuring some of her painful childhood memories.

Loneliness

While at the hospital, Tammy's only visitors were Betty and her dad. When she returned home from the hospital, the occasional visits with her mother did not resume. Tammy was not allowed to see her mom at all. Somehow, however, she managed to sneak a few brief visits at a bar in the Crossroads Mall across the street from where she lived. Mary and her husband frequented there, probably in hopes of seeing Tammy.

School brought little reprieve from the harshness of Tammy's life. The other students teased her and called her "Boll weevil" after the ugly bug that feeds on cotton plants. She was horrified by the nickname and withdrew even more. She didn't have any friends to speak of, and she was the last one picked for team games.

No one at school seems to have questioned Tammy's haggard appearance or anxious, withdrawn behavior. If anyone had seen the back of her thighs, they would have known about the beatings, but these were covered by pants or heavy tights. If anyone at school suspected that anything was wrong at home, they did not say so.

June, the housekeeper, knew that the girls were confined to their bedroom. She picked up the plates of food that were delivered to their room. She may not have been fully aware of the frequent beatings, but she knew that things were not as they should be. She was paid well for her services, and she kept quiet. She had a sick mother and needed the money. She did feel sorry for the girls, however, and was kind to them. When Betty was not home, she allowed them to play outside for a while after school. When she delivered meals to her mother, she took the girls along. They had to crouch down in the backseat of the car, so the neighbors wouldn't see the little white heads. It was too dangerous for them to be seen in the black neighborhood of North Omaha in the nineteen sixties.

The babysitter, Mrs. Hansen, also knew that things were not right. Every Friday night was date night. Channing and Betty went dancing at NASR's Lounge. Mrs. Hansen stayed overnight and watched them on Saturday. They got a little more freedom then to move about the house and maybe watch TV. For very brief times, when they were certain it wouldn't be discovered, she and June allowed the girls to go outside to swing or even to play at the neighbor's house for a little while.

On the weekends, when Channing and Betty went dancing, no furniture was damaged. The girls never got punished on Fridays or Saturdays.

Additional Abuse

Besides the usual, predictable abuse, Tammy faced some outstanding experiences that sent shocks through her system. One time Dad and Betty took a short vacation to Florida. Betty's daughter Julie stayed with the girls. On a Saturday while the parents were gone, Julie let out a loud scream and called for Tammy to come downstairs. Julie grabbed her by the hair and drug her over to a vinyl record, showing her a scratch on the label. As punishment for the supposed offense, Julie threw Tammy on the ground and smeared a used sanitary pad in her face. She then made Tammy hold a barbell over her head for the remainder of the day. If Tammy slumped down, Julie beat her with her crutches. For lunch that day, Tammy got a can of dogfood.

While Tammy was being punished in other parts of the house, Kim was alone upstairs in the bedroom. The house was eerily quiet. She feared that she had been abandoned. Finally, Dad and Betty returned. The girls went out for supper with the family, but instead of rejoicing in their father's presence, they were forced, in the restaurant, to confess to scratching the record and other crimes which they had not committed.

During the brief times that Tammy was outside on the swings or looking up at the sky while waiting for the school bus, she sometimes cried from her heart to God, "Why don't you do something? You know I am innocent and don't deserve this treatment. Where are you?"

Once Tammy tried to run away. She went to the house of a girl she knew down the street. The girl's parents were clients of her father. They didn't ask what was wrong. They called her father, and he came and brought her home.

The Big Night

When Tammy was eleven years old, she started playing flute in the school band. Towards the end of the school year in her sixth grade, she had a concert. It was an exciting event. She had a little opportunity to shine, a little life outside the four walls of her room, and a little interaction with family. Her grandfather, Aunt Cheryl, and Uncle Rusty were in town, visiting from South Dakota.

When Tammy got home from school that beautiful, summer day, the housekeeper, thinking Betty would be gone for a while, allowed the girls to play outside for a bit. Betty came home, found them swinging, and sent them inside to their room immediately.

As a very rare treat, probably because Grandpa, Cheryl, and Rusty were there, Tammy and Kim were allowed to eat with the family on the night of the concert. After supper, Tammy went to her room to change into her band uniform, a blue skirt and new white shirt. Her grandpa and other family members had already left for the concert. While Tammy was in her room, she heard a scream from the hallway, "My diamond bracelet! My diamond bracelet is gone!"

Tammy's heart sank, knowing what was likely to follow. Moments later, her dad burst into the room, his face red with anger. He beat her mercilessly, throwing her from one side of the room to the other and ripping her clothes. He tightly gripped her neck and pounded her against the wall with her feet off the floor. She feared she would die.

Finally, he stopped torturing her and asked, "What do you want from me?"

Tammy said, "I want to see my mom."

"What do you really want?" he asked again.

"I want to live with my mom."

She would get to.

Tammy's blue skirt and band shirt were torn. She was black and blue all over, scared, sore, and very alone. Kim wasn't allowed to be with her for a week. The family didn't want Kim to see Tammy's bruises. Tammy missed her sister deeply, and her heart was broken, but she did have a hope. Her mother would be her salvation!

It is better to trust in the Lord than to put confidence in man.
—Psalm 118:8-9

CHAPTER 3

A Rude Awakening

When Channing divorced her, Mary moved into an apartment in downtown Omaha. Though she didn't drink much herself, she did hang out at a nearby tavern. She purchased drinks for her dog, a Boxer who loved beer. It wasn't long before she met Ivan Kucera.

Ivan was a hard-working, beer-loving Bohemian. He was drawn to the mysterious and beautiful woman, and it is much to his credit that he not only married her, but that he stayed married for over twenty-two years and took care of Mary. He didn't have the knowledge of God, and he didn't have the answers for the troubles of life, but he did have a kind heart, and he took on the role of a father to Mary's children.

Ivan worked long days at the power plant. He stopped at the bar after work for a few drinks and got home late. On days off, he started drinking early and drank a case of Falstaff throughout the day. He did a little cooking here and there and a minimal amount of cleaning. Tammy's brother, Mick, followed Ivan's example. He was a teenager, trying to drown his own troubles in substance abuse. Mary did nothing. She slept days and stayed awake at night watching TV and doing crossword puzzles.

Culture Shock

When Tammy moved in with her mom on July 4, 1970, she lost the wicked stepmother and stepsisters, but she had to work like Cinderella. She had been incredibly isolated throughout her eleven years. Now she had to grow up fast. She had lived much of her life in a room with only her younger sister as a companion. She had limited interactions at school and very few stimulating ones at home. She barely even watched TV. She knew almost nothing about the realities of life. Now she was thrown into a shockingly different world with challenges she could never have dreamed of.

There was no housekeeper at Mom's. Tammy quickly learned that if anything was going to get done, she would have to be the doer of it. She got up and got ready for school shortly after her mom went to bed. When she got home from school, she made coffee for her mom who had slept all day. She sat on her mom's bed and listened to her chatter about nothing for an hour or more while she drank her coffee. Then Tammy did the dishes, made supper, did her homework, and went to bed.

Mary had epilepsy, a result of having had encephalitis as a teenager. Violent and scary seizures wracked her frame several times a month. Her behavior when not having an epileptic attack was just as disturbing. It was completely erratic and unpredictable. Living with her was even more stressful than dealing with the regular but structured beatings that Tammy had endured from her dad. Tammy never knew when her mom was going to fly into a rage or what was going to set her off.

When Mary was overcome by angry passion, she might throw a hot cup of coffee in Tammy's face, tear every last thing off the wall, or tip over the furniture. Once she knocked over a heavy metal hutch full of dishes. When enraged, she became strong and could exert more power than her slight frame would suggest. Tammy's life, far from being saved by the move to her mother's house, became absorbed by the impossible task of trying to keep her stormy mother pacified.

After Tammy had been at her mom's house for a few months, as the Christmas holiday was nearing, she was awakened one night from sleep by loud cries from the bathroom. She got up to see what was going on, but Ivan sent her back to her room. She heard her mom yelling, "I want Tammy!"

Finally, Ivan came and got Tammy and told her that her mother wanted to see her. Tammy walked into the bathroom and got the shock of her life. There was blood everywhere. Her mother had locked herself in the bathroom and slit both her wrists. Ivan had broken in. He used belts to put tourniquets on her arms, but she had fought him. In the struggle, blood had splattered all over the walls and the fixtures of the bathroom. The bloody horror stamped an unforgettable picture into Tammy's memory. The depth of her mother's mental instability gripped her young heart. There was no salvation here.

Mary was taken to the hospital, drugged, and sent back home again. This cycle continued throughout her life with attempts at suicide occurring consistently about every two years.

Little Sister

The following summer, Tammy's dad took her out for supper. She had not seen him since she had moved a year earlier. Over the past few years, Channing had had three heart attacks. Attempting to cut back on work, he had doubled the prices for his veterinary services. So renowned, however, was he, that his business actually increased with the higher rates, and he had twice as much work. At the age of 41, he decided to sell his practice. He and Betty were planning to move to Minnesota where he could spend his days fishing for muskies. He had a question for Tammy. "Would you like your sister to come live with you?"

Would she? Of course she would! She missed Kim intensely. She asked Ivan and her mom, and they agreed that Kim could live with them.

On July 31, 1971, Channing dropped an excited seven-year-old girl off at his ex-wife's house. How glad Kim was to be moving in with her sister!

Somehow, in Mary's irrational thinking, Kim reminded her of Betty. She soon regretted allowing her youngest daughter to move in with her. She looked at Tammy and sneered, "Why did you make me take her?" When she looked at Kim, she mouthed hatred. Her face wrinkled and showed the violent resentment that she felt toward the innocent girl.

More than once Tammy built a barricade to prevent her mother from attacking her little sister. One time, Tammy piled furniture against the bedroom door, so Mary couldn't open it. Mary got in anyway and tore up their bedroom. With Mick's help, the girls escaped, but when they returned to their room, it looked like a tornado had gone through.

Mick often had friends over to the house. One time, after visiting for a while with Mary and Ivan, Mick and his buddies went upstairs. Ivan was sleeping off his drink in a living room chair. Mary was unhappy about being left out of the party. When Kim went to say goodnight, Mary threw her artificial leg at her. The girls ran to the attic and locked the door. Mick and his friends held Mary back from going up the stairs. It took all six of them to hold her down. All night the girls cowered in the attic, listening to banging, crashing, and screaming downstairs. Finally, a doctor came over to tranquilize Mary. When they saw their mom next, she had a black eye, and the house was destroyed. As always when Mary went on her rampages, Tammy and Kim cleaned up the mess.

Another time, when Tammy opened the refrigerator, something fell out. Her mother flew into a rage. Mary grabbed a jar of salad dressing and hit Tammy on the top of her head with

A Rude Awakening

it, causing a large, bleeding gouge. When Tammy went to ER to have stitches, she lied about how she got the cut. The hospital staff suspected she was lying, but there wasn't much they could do. They allowed Tammy to maintain her story.

When Mary was at her worst, the police had to be called. On one occasion, it took three policemen to get Mary into the backseat of the patrol car. In the process, Mary bit one of the officers. The police took Mary to the hospital mental ward. As usual, she came home with new medication.

Mary took pills for epilepsy and for mental illness. When her medication came, she was in danger of taking it all at once. On a few occasions, she did. One afternoon when Tammy got home from high school, she discovered that Mary had taken five hundred pills. There was a white paper on the bedside and death on Mary's face. Tammy called Ivan who called the ambulance. The paramedics had to slap her in the face to wake her. She was on life support in the hospital for a long time. When she began to recover, she called Tammy from the hospital and angrily yelled, "Why didn't you let me die?"

To avoid going home after school, the girls frequently joined Ivan at the Monkey Mountain Bar near where they lived. They would have cheese popcorn, beef jerky, and Pepsi for supper. They played foosball and pool and hung out, away from the tensions of home. The bartender worked with Ivan at the coal plant and knew how crazy his wife was. He pitied the girls.

A neighbor also had compassion on the girls and invited Tammy and Kim over on weekends to help with the baby. The girls were paid to babysit, but the main motive of their kind acquaintance was to give them a reprieve from their turbulent homelife.

Church

Tammy fought to survive and to make the best of her life. Her most cherished memories were from the year she had spent in South Dakota. While at her Aunt Cheryl's, she had gone to church regularly. Living at Mom and Ivan's place, she now had the freedom to attend church again. Rain or shine, she and Kim got up on Sunday mornings, while their parents were sleeping, and walked together to Catholic mass. Their butcher, Mr. Pateidl, was there. He kept a tea cup Chihuahua in his butcher apron. At church the Chihuahua was tucked inside a pocket of his trench coat. He befriended the girls, and they sat with him in the sanctuary. It was a healthy connection with sane and friendly society.

Since the girls did the laundry, they often had a little change, gleaned from Ivan's pockets. They used it to buy candy at the corner store. Next to the store was a lively, gospel-singing church. The walls of the store rocked in time with the loud, energetic music. It sounded so different from the quiet Catholic church that they were used to. Each had its allurements. Tammy knew that God had the answers she needed, but how could she find Him?

Tammy was a victim, but she was also a sinner. She allowed her victimhood to justify wrong attitudes that were buried so deeply in her soul that she didn't even realize they were there until much later. Meanwhile, she did what all dwellers on the earth do. She tried to hide her pain in the pleasures of sin for a season, without giving due regard to her Creator. She made friends at school with girls in the rough, partying crowd, and she did what they did. There were others with higher moral standards. She noticed girls who carried their Bibles and seemed different from the popular kids. She would have been glad to talk with them if they had talked to her, but they were in another world. Tammy was more comfortable with the wild crowd, where she knew she was accepted.

Sickness

In her junior year of high school, Tammy went to a concert with some friends. While there, she went to the bathroom by herself. There was a group of girls in the restroom who made her uncomfortable. Scared, she left right away, without washing her hands. She joined her friends and smoked a joint with them. This combination of activities, never a good idea, was calamitous for Tammy, whose immune system was already worn away by years of intense stress.

Tammy got very sick. She spent hours in the bathroom every morning and often missed class. By this time, Tammy had confided in one of her teachers and a counselor, so they knew about her homelife. They could see that she was ill. The stress she endured was wearing out her body. She was gaunt, and her skin was starting to turn yellow. Her advocates at school urged her to tell her mother and get medical help.

Finally, one early spring day, Tammy noticed that her pants were stained a bright orange, and she went to the school nurse. The nurse told Tammy that she was going to call Mary. If Tammy wouldn't tell her parents about her ill health, the nurse would. Near the end of April, Tammy finally told her parents, and Ivan took her to the doctor. She was diagnosed with hepatitis A, probably contracted at the concert where she had been smoking with unwashed hands.

The hepatitis should have cleared up on its own in a couple of months. The jaundice had improved, but other symptoms were not relieved, so on July 4, 1976, she was admitted to Immanuel Hospital for more testing. Despite numerous tests, the medical professionals could not determine what was wrong. She had to go to St. Joseph's Hospital for one more test.

When she walked into the old hospital building, Tammy was overwhelmed by memories of the year she had spent there. It had seemed pleasant enough at the time, but the trying life she had lived since then, the uncertainty she faced on account of her ill health, and the fears she had of the upcoming procedure all conspired together to weigh her soul with anxiety.

Tammy was diagnosed with pancreatitis. Her counselors from school knew it was caused by stress. They all urged her to move out of her mother's house. Tammy agreed, but she didn't know where to go. Desperate, she called her dad. "Can I move back with you and Betty?" He said no.

Tammy had been working at a pizza shop. She had taken some time off to deal with her health issues, but as soon as she was able, she returned to work. Throughout her senior year, she went to school in the morning until noon. Then she worked afternoons from one to nine daily for a hotel reservation company. She worked weekends at the pizza shop.

In the fall of 1976, during Tammy's last year of school, Mary had another blow-up. Tammy moved out. She stayed with Ivan's sister for a while. Then she lived with a friend until she was able to get a place that really felt like home.

For to be carnally minded is *death; but to be spiritually minded is life and peace.* —Romans 8:6

CHAPTER 4

A Place to Call Home

When Phil Kleymann sauntered into the pizza shop, Tammy recognized him from high school. Everyone knew Phil. At six foot, two inches, his lanky frame stood out among the students. Because of his easy-going and friendly personality, he was well-liked, and his cartoon drawings were on many of the lockers. Tammy already admired him from a distance. He was tall, dark, and handsome. He didn't offer any worldly sophistication or glamor, but she wasn't looking for that. She had witnessed enough of it through her father's high-class associations, and it did not entice her. All she wanted was love and security, and maybe a little fun. This boy, with his curly head, sparkling eyes, and mischievous smile, was absolutely dreamy!

Phil came from a hard-working, middle-class family. He was employed by a property management company, so he was often at the pizza shop, sweeping the parking lot. He came in for pizza and to chat with Tammy's co-worker Mike.

Tammy suggested to Mike that on a weekend, he call Phil to go out with him and his girlfriend and take Tammy along. Mike agreed. He picked up his girlfriend, then got Phil. He drove to Mary and Ivan's where Tammy lived and told Phil to knock on the door. Tammy was ready to go.

Tammy greatly enjoyed that evening, August 4, 1976. She and Phil walked in the stubble on fallow corn fields, Phil barefoot, as usual. When she got home, Tammy wistfully told Kim, "I'm going to marry him some day."

Phil and Tammy had been dating a week or so when Phil told Tammy that he and a friend named Dan were going on a fishing trip to Leech Lake, Minnesota

"Leech Lake!" Tammy proclaimed excitedly. "My dad lives there. He catches fish that are five feet long!"

Phil and his friend laughed at her.

At Leech Lake, Phil and Dan went into a famous tackle shop on the lake. Dan asked the guy at the counter, "How can I catch a musky?"

"If you want to catch musky, come in after lunch," the clerk told him. "There's a guy named Doc who comes in. He is an expert musky fisherman, and he will gladly give you some pointers."

Dan wanted to wait and talk to Doc, but Phil was anxious to get some fish for eating. He wasn't looking for trophies. "No way," he told his friend, jabbing him in the side. "We need to get walleye fishing!"

The two young guys went fishing, but they didn't catch anything. They had been planning on eating their catch, but they were reduced to living on boiled crawdads and the generosity of the neighbors.

When Phil got back to Omaha, Tammy pulled out a box of magazine clippings to show him. Every outdoor magazine that Phil had heard of was represented. Each had pictures of a small man wearing glasses and golf shorts, holding a huge musky. The headlines read, "Doc Breaks North American Record!" or "Doc Lands Massive Musky."

"Doc! Your dad is Doc?" exclaimed Phil. "I could have met your dad, but I was too much in a hurry to get out fishing!"

Home

Phil and Tammy were dating in September 1976 when Tammy decided to move out of her mother's house. Phil told her he would find them a place to live. He and a friend went together on an apartment, and Tammy moved in with them in January, 1977. The guys paid the rent, and Tammy did the cooking and cleaning and kept the apartment stocked with food and necessary items. How glorious it was for her to get away from the chaos of her mother's house and finally have a place worth coming home to!

Although their arrangement was not done God's way, Phil provided Tammy with more stability and consistency than she had experienced up to that point in her life. She knew that she could count on him. He disappeared during bird hunting season, but she understood. When pheasant season opened, Phil would bring Tammy a dozen roses with a note that said, in effect, "See ya at the end of season."

Phil and Tammy lived together in the apartment with another friend for over three years. They led a careless life, roaming the woods, dealing drugs, getting high, drinking, and going to the bar together. One summer day while they were camping in Fremont, Nebraska, they went for a walk. Phil stopped on a railroad track, looked at Tammy, and said, "We should get married." Tammy readily agreed. They set the wedding for the following May.

Phil wanted to save face and make things look good. It would not do to be living with a girl when he got married! He moved back home with his parents.

Around the same time that Phil and Tammy decided to get married, Kim called. Tammy had told her that if it got too hard to live with their mother, Tammy would find a place where they could live together.

By strength of personality, Tammy was an overcomer. Despite her grueling schedule, hellish upbringing, and stressful life, she had graduated from high school. She was making her way in the world. She worked days for a stock brokerage firm, and she waitressed on the weekends. Trying to save up for her wedding, she also held parties for home decor and babysat when she could. Nonetheless, it took some searching to find an apartment that Tammy could afford in Kim's school district. Eventually she found a place that was willing to take a chance on them. Most of the other tenants in the building were single women, all of them relatively young, except the lady directly under Tammy and Kim.

Tammy got to know the other young women in the building and befriended one of them. She asked Tammy if she had met the older woman, Louise, who lived downstairs. "Stay away from her," she said, "or you'll get a lecture." Tammy took this advice and kept her distance from Louise.

Phil technically lived with his parents, but he was often at Tammy's apartment. He worked nights and she days. They had bought a stereo as well as other items in anticipation of starting a home together. Friends came over and spent time with them, playing music, drinking or doing drugs, and just hanging out. Tammy's brother, Mick, and Phil's brothers were regular guests.

Joe

Phil's oldest brother, Joe, had been a speed junkie, racing cars and motorcycles. He spent every weekend in the garage, working on his race car. In August, 1980, Phil and Tammy heard that something had happened to Joe. He had quit drinking, smoking, and cussing, and he was talking about selling his racecar. They were stunned.

Phil and his brothers were worried about Joe. They thought he was in a cult and in need of deprogramming. They held a big party, intending to get him drunk. He came over, but he didn't drink. They stuck a cold beer under his nose. To everyone's surprise, he declined it. They pressed him, but he said, "I found something better." The Lord Jesus had set him free from his old lifestyle, and he was ready to talk about it with all who would listen.

Joe had worked with a Christian who was mocked for not participating in the dark activities that the others thought were fun. Joe realized that, though his co-worker was ridiculed, this guy was the only one in the place who was truly happy. He gave Joe a book on Bible prophecy. Joe read the book and started to wonder about the things of God. His roommate, Kevin, had been given a Bible by some random Christians he had met while hiking in the mountains, but he had left it unused. Joe dug through Kevin's drawers and found it. Hungrily, he devoured the words of life. He read about the cross of Christ, and the story gripped his heart like it never had before. He realized that Jesus had died for his sins. He broke down in tears and surrendered his life to Christ. Soon he was telling others the good news. When his brothers showed no interest, he prayed for them.

Phil didn't understand his brother's newfound religion, and he didn't like having the status quo overturned. He and the other brothers mocked Joe and kept pressing him to drink. Nothing moved him.

Tammy, on the other hand, was all ears. She mulled these things over in her heart without saying much. A little later, she ran into Joe's roommate at the laundromat. She knew Kevin as someone who liked to party and seemed to live for nothing else. She asked him if he had heard about Joe and his craziness about religion. Kevin looked at her and said, "Tammy, you need to listen to him."

Kevin had gotten saved too! Tammy's world was reeling. If even Kevin could be changed, there must be something in this Jesus stuff!

Cowboys

Phil and Tammy and whatever friends decided to join them always went to Cowboys Bar on the weekends. The last Friday night of January, 1981, Tammy knew Phil was trying to reach her to make plans. He had her car and was going to pick her up to go to Cowboys, but she didn't know what time, and her phone wasn't working. She went to the neighbor's apartment to borrow the phone. Her friend wasn't home. Tammy tried the other apartments. No one was home but Louise. There was nothing to do, but to knock.

Ask, and it shall be given you; seek, and ye shall find; knock, and it shall be opened unto you. —Matthew 7:7

CHAPTER 5

Grandma

The little woman who answered the door when Tammy knocked was Louise Hamilton. She had a soft voice, but a firm grip on God's Word. She had been a widow for about four years. Her children and grandchildren, who loved her dearly, were in and out of her apartment frequently. Phil and Tammy soon came to love her, too, and to call her *Grandma*.

Louise had been born in Iowa in 1909. She had two siblings, eleven and twelve years older than she was. Her father had led a wild life of drinking and carousing, but before Louise was born, he had changed completely. He started to speak about Christ, and he no longer played music for dances. He died when Louise was only a year old. She never got to hear him pray, but God did.

Louise's widowed mother was barely able to make ends meet. She washed clothes and ironed for wealthier families, leaving Louise in the care of her teenage sister from early morning until dark. Louise's sister did not treat her well. She would promise their mother that she would not hit Louise, but she was burdened with trying circumstances herself, and her good intentions never lasted very long.

When Louise was eleven, her sister married. Their brother had been running the streets for years and getting into trouble. Their mom was often in court and doing what she could to reclaim her son from crime and drug use. This left Louise very much alone, in a cold house, without proper meals, and with no one to talk to. She often walked by the home of a large family and saw them sitting around a table eating together, and she longed for a family. She felt like she never belonged to anything or anybody.

At some point a stepfather came into the picture, but this was no improvement to Louise's situation. He drank heavily and was very difficult to live with.

Louise met Harry Hamilton when she was a young teenager. She was dating someone else at the time and had arranged for another girl to go along with her and her date and his friend Harry. Harry took an interest in Louise immediately and began to pursue her, leaving her original date out of the picture.

Louise was seventeen, and Harry was nearly done with electronics school, when he urged her to run off with him to get married. At first, she said no, but as she reflected on her miserable homelife, she decided that marriage to Harry was her best option. As soon as Louise agreed to marry him, Harry drove to a town in Iowa where Louise was in a basketball tournament. After the game, they drove together to a neighboring county and married without parental permission, despite Louise being under age.

Because of financial hardships, Harry and Louise had moved into a boarding house in Ottumwa, Iowa. It was run by Christians, Orville and Kate Smith. At first, Louise was uneasy about the gospel texts on the wall, and she avoided talking to the Smiths. Eventually, Kate found an opportunity to tell her timid boarder about the love of Christ and the beauty of His gift for her. Kate painted a word picture of the crucifixion that moved Louise's heart, and she gladly embraced the love of Christ for her soul. She shared the good news with Harry. He resisted at first, but when she convinced him to read John 3:16, he also believed in the Savior.

Their newfound love for Christ drew Harry and Louise into a closer bond with one another, and they became a team proclaiming the gospel. Not only did God give Louise the family that her heart craved, He also used her and Harry to lead her mother, sister, and brother to Christ. Even her stepfather professed faith in Christ before he died.

In 1932, Harry and Louise moved to Omaha, Nebraska. Louise had a vision for taking in boarders as Kate and Orville had done. In answer to her prayers, the Lord provided a large house at 1616 Military Avenue and a dining table that seated sixteen people. They rented rooms to students from the electronics school where Harry taught. They also took in foster children. Many of the young people, both from the foster system and the school, were led to faith in Christ by the ministry and hospitality of Harry and Louise Hamilton.

The Hamiltons were simple, common people, working quietly behind the scenes. The world scarcely took note of them, but they were on fire with the power of the gospel of Jesus Christ. They followed Him, and He made them fishers of men.

Bill Fear

A handsome and eloquent insurance agent, who had recently believed on Jesus as his savior, started attending the church that Harry and Louise belonged to. The Hamiltons invited Bill Fear into their home. Bill was intrigued to meet people who actually lived their life by the Bible, and he followed them as they followed Christ. He had been extremely successful as an insurance salesman, and for five years in a row had obtained an award as the top salesman in his district. The year after meeting the Hamiltons, he was, as usual, the keynote speaker at the annual conference for his company. When he got up to speak, instead of giving his customary self-help speech, he plainly told his audience that he could no longer pressure people to buy life insurance because it was not in keeping with his faith in his Lord and Savior, Jesus Christ. He told them he had been born again, and he resigned.

Bill Fear and his ambitious companions in Omaha went in opposite directions. By resigning from his prominent and lucrative position, Bill assured himself a life of obscurity, but his faith in Christ secured an eternal inheritance that far outweighs all the benefits of the wealthiest men on earth. Bill earned a modest living selling office equipment.

Bill was like a son to Harry and Louise. Indeed, he married their daughter, Mary, and became their son-in-law.

Bill and Mary Fear had three daughters. They wanted their girls to experience the love of Christ and to walk in the freedom of the gospel. Louise, who was widowed in 1977, shared Bill and Mary's concern for the spiritual well-being of her grandchildren and their friends. She, Bill, and Mary worked together to reach out to the young people in their church.

Many of the young people, who had grown up in Christian homes, had placed their faith in the forms of religion without having assurance of true faith in Christ Jesus. They were going along with what they had been taught, but they lacked vibrant, living faith. Bill and Mary and Louise were more concerned about the reality of each person's conversion than about appearances. They taught the young people to trust in the Word of God, not in an experience, and to place their faith in the Lord Jesus Christ, not in a doctrine or in the accepted forms of their own denomination. This was upsetting to those who were comfortable in their traditions, but it was blessed of God. Many young people were saved and strengthened in faith.

When a soul was struggling, he or she was often brought to Grandma. She opened the Bible and helped seeking souls to find the Scriptures that applied to each person's circumstances.

She would ask people to read from the Bible and would hold the reader to the text. After someone read a portion, she would ask, "What does God say?"

The answer may be a general truth, such as "Jesus died on the cross," but Grandma would press for specifics in the text at hand, making sure that people were hearing from God through His Word, not just repeating human platitudes.

Besides personal work whenever people were brought to her apartment, Grandma went out fishing for souls in the community. She went swimming and shared the gospel with the other women at the pool. She was involved in church activities almost every day of the week. Though she could and did drive, her daughter or her granddaughters and their friends often picked her up for Bible studies and prayer meetings. Thus, there was a lot of coming and going from her apartment.

Young People Upstairs

When some rowdy young people moved into the apartment above Louise's apartment, marijuana fumes came down through the vents. Troubled by the loud music, Louise would sometimes knock on their door and gently ask, "Please turn the music down." Usually someone did turn down the volume, at least for a while.

Louise knew where to take her troubles. "Lord," she prayed, "You'll either have to save these kids, or get me a new apartment."

He that winneth souls is wise. —Proverbs 11:30

CHAPTER 6

The Hairs of Her Head

Tammy needed to borrow a phone. She hesitated about going to Louise's apartment. She had been warned that the old lady would give her a lecture. She tried every other door in the building. No one was home, so she knocked on Louise's door. A kind woman in her seventies opened the door. Tammy asked to use the phone, and Louise let her in. After Tammy arranged with Phil to pick her up later that evening, she hung up. Louise pulled out a chair and asked her to visit. Tammy sat down and chatted about her life. She was engaged, getting married in May. Her sister lived with her. Louise seemed genuinely interested. Tammy politely asked her, "What about you? It looks like you have a big family. Young people are always coming and going from the apartment."

"Those are my friends. Some are grandchildren. I have been a widow for years."

"You must be very lonely!"

"Oh, honey," Louise replied, "I'm not lonely, because I'm never alone. I have my best friend here with me all the time."

Tammy looked around, confused. Who was she talking about? Grandma Louise told her about the Lord Jesus. Tammy stayed at Grandma's apartment for two hours, listening to her talk about the wonders of knowing Christ. When she left, Louise told her to read the gospel of John and gave her some pamphlets with Bible verses to look up.

Phil was upstairs. He had been waiting for Tammy for some time. She went with him to the bar as usual, but the whole time they were there, she was thinking about the things she had heard from Louise. "This is what I have been looking for for so many years," she told herself. When she got home at 1:30 in the morning, she started reading the Bible and the pamphlets that Louise had given her. Over the next few days, she absorbed the Scriptures. She read the Bible during her hour-long bus ride to and from work and during her lunch break.

On the following Wednesday, Louise called and asked Tammy if she had been reading the Bible and if she had any questions. Yes, she had questions, so she went downstairs to talk.

As a means of explaining the horrible circumstances in which she had grown up, Tammy had adopted a belief in reincarnation. She theorized that she had been very wicked in a past life. She was now paying her penance. Her current life was her purgatory, and she would go to heaven when she died.

Grandma said, "You will not find purgatory in the Bible."

Tammy was shocked.

"The Bible says, 'It is appointed unto men once to die, but after this the judgment' (Heb. 9:27). Tammy, have you accepted what God has done for you on the cross? Have you been born again?"

"No."

"Do you know what that means? That means you have rejected what God's Son has done for you. This is the one sin that God will not forgive—denying His Son. For that you will go to hell."

"This life has been hell," Tammy said.

"No, this is not hell," Grandma said. She opened her Bible and read Luke 16 about the rich man in hell. He was burning in torments and begged for Lazarus to get him a drop of water. This small comfort was denied him.

Tammy was absolutely petrified. Hell was real. She was rejecting the only way of salvation.

Louise had invited Tammy to a Bible study the following evening. Tammy wanted to go, but she had already scheduled a home party and wouldn't be free. When she got home, she had a message on her phone. The hostess for her party hadn't been able to get any guests, so she was cancelling the event.

"Oh, praise the Lord!" was Louise's joyous response when Tammy called to tell her that she would be free on Thursday after all.

At work the next day, Tammy looked around at the friends she had partied with. Were they all going to hell? She knew almost every one of them was guilty of the same sins that she committed on a regular basis. It made her sick to her stomach to think about it. "I have to get this answered," she thought to herself. "Where am I going?" Worrying about Phil's reaction intensified her nausea. She knew that he would not want to go to the Bible study.

When Phil got to her apartment that evening, Tammy told him that she wanted to go to the Bible study.

"Are you nuts?" Phil asked. "Get dressed up. We'll go anywhere. Cowboys, a movie, whatever, but I am not going to that Bible study!"

The phone rang. Tammy said to Phil, "You answer it. It's going to be her. I'm not answering it."

Phil answered. "Uh, OK, we'll be there," he said.

Furious with himself, he said to Tammy, "I'll go tonight, but I'm never doing this again."

The Study

When Phil and Tammy walked in to the Bible study, Tammy immediately recognized Louise's granddaughter, Marion. She was one of the girls who had carried a Bible with her in high school! Around thirty-five young people were present. Many of them knew Phil and Tammy from school; some had partied with them. Tammy recognized a few of them. One rowdy guy made her think to herself, "If *he* can get saved, I can!"

During the Bible study, something was said that made Tammy sincerely ask about Jesus, "Please somebody tell me, how did He know me? He lived over 1900 years ago. I was nowhere in existence 1900 years ago."

One young man looked at Tammy and said, "God is all-knowing. You're limiting his power, and you don't have the right to do that."

Then, Bill Fear quoted Matthew 10:30, "But the very hairs of your head are all numbered."

He said to Tammy, "That's how well God knows you. He knows every hair on your head."

With her mind spinning, Tammy thought to herself, "I am where I am because of Tammy. I graduated high school. I work three jobs. I'm getting married." She put her hand to her head. "How many hairs are on my head? I don't know. I don't know myself as well as I think I do. I am where I am because of me, but me is not going to get me to heaven."

With those thoughts, Tammy put herself at the foot of the cross. She saw the Lord Jesus dying for her. "The very hairs of my head are numbered," she thought. "That's how well He knew me." Her countenance changed. People in the room could see the light come on and the peace of God fill her. She looked at Grandma Louise who was sitting to her right. Tammy whispered to her, "I'm so glad I came tonight."

Grandma whispered to the person next to her, "She just got saved." The news spread all around the room until it got to Phil and stopped. Phil was angry. He made objections about Pygmies in Africa and whatever else he could think of.

The young people approached Tammy after the study and asked her what happened. She hardly knew what to say, but she knew she had peace. She knew Jesus had died for her. And she knew the very hairs of her head were numbered.

Tammy became a new creation in Christ Jesus on February 5, 1981. She received a whole new perspective on life. She demanded privacy from Phil, which surprised her as much as it angered him. She didn't want to go to the bar anymore. She went skating with her Christian friends instead, leaving Phil to go out with the guys. When she went to a movie with Phil, she found the satanic overtones so disturbing that she walked out and asked him never to take her to that kind of show again.

Desires of the Heart

It wasn't just that Tammy no longer wanted the party life. Her conversion went deeper than that. She wanted God. She wanted her family life to be different than the one she had grown up with. Somehow she knew that she needed God to be involved in every aspect of her being if she was going to accomplish that.

Phil had rescued Tammy from the stressful and chaotic life she had experienced at her mom's. He provided her with companionship and security. He had given her a reason to go home for the first time in seventeen years. She loved him for it. But he was just a man. The Lord Jesus knew every hair on her head. He had forgiven her of her sins and received her into His family for eternity. She wanted Him to be central to everything in her life going forward.

Phil felt jilted. Tammy was changing. The two of them were going in different directions, and the relationship was not going to work. Tammy begged Phil to sit down and talk and read the Bible with her. He grabbed the Bible out of her arms and chucked it across the room. With angry words, he left in a huff, slamming the door on his way out.

Kim pleaded with Tammy, "Look what you are doing to you and Phil!"

Grandma heard the commotion upstairs and called Tammy. In tears, Tammy went downstairs. "I've lost him," she wailed.

"Where's your faith?" Grandma gently asked.

"I don't have any," bawled Tammy.

"What's most important to you?" Grandma asked.

"I want a good marriage. I want my children to be in a happy home. If it's not with Phil, that's OK. I just want a Christian family."

Grandma got out her Bible. She opened to Psalm 37 and read, "Fret not . . . trust in the Lord." She told Tammy to claim verse 4, "Delight thyself also in the Lord; and he shall give thee the desires of thine heart."

"Let's pray," Grandma said.

Tammy prayed, "If this is the man you want me to spend the rest of my life with, you will save his soul. If he's not, I will wait for the one who is."

After prayer, Grandma devised a plan. Tammy would spend the night with her new Christian friends. They would pray together for Phil and ask God specifically to send him to Grandma's apartment.

The effectual fervent prayer of a righteous man availeth much.
—James 5:16

CHAPTER 7

God or Me

There was absolutely no way Phil was going to Grandma's apartment. He didn't know about the prayer, of course, but Louise Hamilton's home was about the last place on earth where he would willingly go.

Phil's upbringing was completely different from Tammy's. He had grown up in a stable, loving family with a secure homelife and a good religious education. There was strict discipline, no fighting, no smoking, no drinking. His vices were learned at school, not at home.

From his father and grandfather, Phil learned to love hunting. At Thanksgiving gatherings, he watched with excitement and wonder as his dad, uncles, and grandpa brought in the pheasants and laid down their guns. He could hardly wait until he was old enough to go along. He saved up his paper route money to buy a shot gun and hounded his dad until he agreed to take him hunting. Phil loved the woods, and his dream was to have a place in the country. Once in a while his parents would talk about getting an acreage. Phil held his breath, hoping it would come to pass.

Phil was a bit of a clown, and he was known at school for his entertaining stories and cartoons. He was a natural story teller, and he kept his boy scout troop entertained at campfires.

When he went to the movies, he would come home and tell the whole story. His dad joked that the family could save a lot of money on movie tickets. Instead of buying everyone a ticket, they could get one for Phil and let him tell the story to everyone else.

Phil took his upbringing for granted. Careless about God and eternity, he didn't value the truths that he had heard from youth, and he was not looking for anything. He loved Tammy, but he did not understand her newfound interest in religion and the Bible. He did not like it. Couldn't she see she was ruining everything?

Tammy wasn't the same person she had been. Phil had reluctantly agreed to go to the Bible study with her, and the girl who came out of that study was not the same one he had walked in with. He walked out with a stranger he didn't recognize. Things had only gotten worse since then.

The Comet

The weekend following Tammy's conversion, she went to a skating party with her new friends. Phil went to the Cowboy's Bar with his brothers, confused and angry about the change in Tammy that had turned his life upside down. At closing time, he picked a fight with a bouncer. Phil was beaten, maced, and thrown into the street. Phil's brothers dragged him by his coat and stuck him behind the wheel of Tammy's Mercury Comet, which he had borrowed. He was in no condition to drive. Mercifully, no serious harm came to him or anyone else, but he ran into a parked car and put some serious dents in Tammy's Comet.

The next morning, being Sunday, Phil sheepishly called Tammy to tell her that he had wrecked her car. Like a true hero, he said, "If it will make you feel any better, I'll go to church with you today." She jumped at the offer. He tried to back pedal by suggesting his family church, but she said, "It was my car. We are going to my church."

Phil was wearing the same stinky jacket that he had worn in the bar. The preacher may have thought he had a fish on a hook, because Phil started tearing up during the service. Unfortunately, nothing from the message penetrated Phil's heart. His tears were the result of the mace residue on his leather jacket.

The Fight

Phil and Tammy were going in different directions. Tammy was walking in the light and seeking God's will for her life. Phil, still very much in the dark, was perturbed about the changes that were being forced upon him. He was more comfortable in the dark, and Tammy was starting to get on his nerves. He felt irritable whenever he was around her.

When Tammy was trying to convince Phil to read the Bible with her, she stunned him by saying, "Phil if we get married, God must be first in our marriage, and we would be second."

This is what infuriated him, so that he grabbed her Bible out of her hand. He threw it across the room, cursing and saying, "They've brainwashed you with this thing!"

That night at work, Phil shared his woes with a friend. The friend advised him to give Tammy an ultimatum. "Tell her, 'It's either me or this God-stuff,'" he said. "There are other fish in the stream. Go out with me tonight."

"Yeah, that's what I'll do," Phil thought. He'd go out with Rick. He would just stop by Tammy's place before going out and give her one last chance. "You can have me or this God stuff!" he would tell her.

As Phil left work, he felt the fear of God grip him like an angry father grabbing him by the back of the neck. "Me or you? Really, Phil?" He was raised in church, and he thought he was

OK with God. Would he dare to set himself up against God? He should at least give Tammy a chance to explain herself.

Phil thought about his brother. Joe's life had been changed by the Bible, just like Tammy's. "What is it they see that I can't see?" he thought. Getting into his car, he remembered being at the Bible study. People tried to explain the Bible to him, but he just pushed it away. He thought to himself, "Maybe you ought to keep your big Irish mouth shut long enough for Tammy to show you in the Bible what it is she sees that I don't see." He decided to stop by the apartment before going out for the night, but instead of giving her an ultimatum, he would give her a chance to talk. And he would listen.

A Light in the Window

When Phil arrived at Tammy's, she was gone. He got back into his car planning to head to the bar. As he drove away, he noticed that every window in the apartment building was dark except one—Louise's. "Of course!" Phil thought, "That's where she is!"

Phil turned around and headed back to the apartment building to look for Tammy at Louise's place. As he walked up the stairs, he coached himself, "Whatever you do, don't go in. She's the cause of all our problems! Have her send Tammy out, but do not get tangled up with that woman."

He knocked, feeling ready for whatever came through the door. A tiny, old woman in a blue dress appeared. She had rosy cheeks, wirerimmed glasses, snow white hair, and a warm smile. Phil asked if Tammy was there.

"No, she's not." There was a pause. Then Louise added, "Would you like to talk?"

Surprising himself, Phil said, "Yes."

"Come on in," she said, and they stepped inside.

Phil expected a lecture. "I'm going to get it," he thought to himself. Louise had smelled his pot smoke. She had heard the loud music, and she had heard the fighting. "Probably she blames me for everything," thought Phil.

Instead of chewing him out, Louise placed a Bible in front of him. She looked at Phil and said, "I suppose you are here because you are wondering what's happened to your brother Joe and to Tammy."

Phil had to admit it. "You're right. I am," he said.

"You know it's real. Do you want to see it in the Bible?" She turned to 2 Corinthians 5:17, "Therefore if any man be in Christ, he is a new creature: old things are passed away; behold, all things are become new."

Grandma had Phil's undivided attention. She then turned him to John 3:3, "Except a man be born again, he cannot see the kingdom of God."

It almost took him out of his seat. He had never heard this before. This explained Tammy and Joe! They had been born again. Grandma and Phil talked for hours. When Phil got up to use the bathroom, Grandma called the girls and told them to keep praying. After more exhortations, she sent Phil up to Tammy's apartment with a Bible and some verses she had written out for him. She told him, "Phil, get alone with God and look these up. If you're serious, He'll show you. He will show you in His Word."

Phil was awakened and interested. He knew he was a sinner in need of salvation. He didn't go out with Rick. He read the Bible until he fell asleep on the couch. When Tammy's brother, Mick, came over in the morning, Phil showed him what he had been reading in the Bible and asked, "Mick, have you ever seen this before?"

Tammy came home midmorning on Saturday. She walked into her apartment and was startled to see both Phil and Mick reading the Bible. Phil looked up long enough to see her stunned expression. He said, "Hey, good morning," and went back to reading. Tammy went straight to her bedroom stunned. The last time they were together, Phil had thrown the Bible across the room. Now he was reading it.

It's Real

There was a Bible study that afternoon. Phil and Mick agreed to go with Tammy. This time Phil wanted to be there. While there, a Christian named Ken Rempel said to Phil, "The Lord is building a house. When the house is ready, he's taking it home. Are you part of that house?"

Phil knew he wasn't. "No, I'm not," he said.

"I'll pray for you," said Ken.

Bill and Mary Fear invited the young people to their house for refreshments after the study. Bill visited with Mick in the front room. Mary took Phil and Tammy to a room which earned the name, "the birthing room" because of the people brought to Christ there. When they settled down in chairs, Mary asked Phil, "What are you thinking?"

"It's real for Joe. It's real for Tammy. It's not real for me yet," Phil said. "I was raised in a religion hearing that Jesus died for our sins, and I believe that. But it's just words on a page. I believe it like I believe that Abraham Lincoln lived and died. It's not a life-changing thing to me. If Jesus would appear and show me that He died for me, I'd get up on the housetop, and I'd preach it to everyone."

Mary said, "I want you to meet someone in the Bible." She turned Phil to the story of Thomas in John 20. Phil read about how Jesus had appeared to His disciples after His resurrection. Thomas wasn't there with the others and hadn't seen Jesus. He declared, "I'll have to see it to believe it."

Phil related to this. "Yeah, I've got you, Thomas, I know exactly where you're at!" he thought.

Eight days later, Jesus appeared again, invited Thomas to touch the nail prints in his hands, and said, "Be not faithless, but believing!"

Thomas cried out, "My Lord, and my God."

Then Phil read verse 29, "Jesus saith unto him, Thomas, because thou hast seen me, thou hast believed: blessed are they that have not seen, and yet have believed."

The light came on. Jesus became a reality to Phil.

Tammy watched Phil's eyes brighten. She saw a weight lift off him. Phil was saved. It was February 17, 1981, twelve days after Tammy's new birth. Tammy was thrilled, not only that Phil was saved, but also to watch the work of God in a soul. She was hooked and wanted more of this kind of fishing!

Meanwhile, Mick was coming to Christ in the other room.

I say unto you, that likewise joy shall be in heaven over one sinner that repenteth. —Luke 15:7

CHAPTER 8

Mick

Tammy's brother, Mick, was nearly six years older than Tammy. He shared with his sister the pain of their unhappy home life. As a toddler, Mick had an unexplained broken ankle, probably the result of abuse from his unstable mother. One day, he found his little sister stone cold in her crib. He ran to his mom. "Mommy, mommy," he cried, "Sandy is cold!" Could his mother have not known of her baby's death before her four-year-old child?

When Mick's mother shot herself in the foot, it made a deep impression on him. He did not know at the time that she had done it to win her husband's sympathy and forestall divorce. She told him that later. But a child feels the insecurity and confusion that he does not understand.

A bright spot in Mick's world of fighting and sorrow was his little sister, Tammy. She was born about a year and a half after Sandy died. Mick would hide in the attic or in the dog's kennel, holding Tammy in his arms. Both were crying, while their parents fought in a nearby room.

Mick was around eleven years old when his parents divorced. He had seen enough of his mother's unfaithfulness to figure out why. The divorce tore at his heart, but as he thought it over and grew in his understanding, he could not blame his dad. He had seen his mom in bed with the milkman. The adulterers had shown no compunction when he walked by the bedroom door. They had just smiled at him.

Mick desperately wanted his dad's love and approval, and he hoped for a happier home life when the family moved to Betty's house. He was quickly disappointed. A learning disability made school difficult for him, and when he asked for help, Betty and her daughters made fun of him. Instead of encouragement or support, he was sent to his room as punishment for his bad grades. By the time he was a teenager, Mick's unmet desire for his dad's affection had ripened into deep resentment. He hated both Betty and his dad. He was old enough to choose where to live, and he chose Mom's.

Teenage Alcoholic

Mick's mother, Mary, had married Ivan Kucera. The first week that Mick lived with Ivan and his mom, he broke up a fight between them. He soon realized that he was living with an unstable mother and an alcoholic stepfather, but he could see no alternative and no solution, and he fell in with their lifestyle. When he visited his sisters, they gave him a note saying that they were being beaten. He knew it. He had already witnessed it, but what was he, a teenage alcoholic, going to do about it?

Mick had no rules or boundaries at Mom and Ivan's house. When Ivan found a pack of Marlboro cigarettes in the bathroom, he knew they were Mick's. Mick tried to deny that they were his, but Ivan smoked Chesterfields. Instead of reprimanding him, Ivan said, "If you are going to smoke, you might as well do it in front of us."

Ivan had the same attitude about drinking. "You might as well do it at home." He procured alcohol for Mick and his friends, making Mick's place a party house for teenagers. This gave Mick a sort of popularity with the wrong type of kids, but it did not fill the deep longing of his soul for true security.

When Mick graduated from high school, he moved out on his own. His sisters felt abandoned again, but he didn't realize that his presence in the home was a support to them. He was tired of his mother's suicide attempts, and he followed Ivan's example of dealing with the stress of life by indulgence in alcohol and other substances.

Drinking and drugs did not give Mick what he was seeking. He was restless and unsatisfied, and he became a wanderer. He went out to Colorado where he stayed for a while with a friend of Ivan's. He found work, but he also found hard drugs, and he partied hard.

One day two hippies showed up at Mick's door. One of them said, "Hey, man, you got any pot?"

Mick said, "Sure," and turned around to get it.

"You're under arrest."

The guys weren't hippies. They were federal agents.

Mick's mom and Ivan trekked to Colorado to bail him out of jail.

After two years in Colorado, Mick wandered the country, working with horses at race tracks in Omaha and other places. He was in the army for a while, took animal science classes at different colleges, and traveled the globe.

Death to Sin

Providentially, Mick was in Omaha in the fall of 1980. He had partied with Phil and his brothers and was friends with all of them. He heard that Joe had changed dramatically. Sure enough, as soon as Joe saw Mick, he talked to him about the Lord Jesus. Mick was intrigued. He went to a youth group with Joe and was surprised to see people having fun without alcohol and pot. Mick wanted healing from the deep hurts of his life, and he talked to Joe about it. Joe told him to ask Jesus into his heart. Mick went up to the altar at a church service and went through the proper formula. He thought going through the motions had saved him, but his life did not change. He was still drinking heavily and smoking pot.

When Tammy talked to him about salvation, Mick told her he had gotten saved too. Tammy said to him, "Ya know Mick, if you died tonight, you would still go to hell!"

Mick thought to himself, "How can she say that?" But she was his little sister, and he let it go.

The morning Mick came to Tammy's apartment and found Phil reading the Bible, political unrest in the Middle East was on his mind. Phil showed him things from the Bible that seemed to pertain to current affairs. This deepened Mick's interest in the Bible. He readily agreed to go to a Bible study that afternoon and to Bill and Mary Fear's house afterward. While Mary was in another room with Phil and Tammy, Mick visited in the living room with Louise Hamilton and Bill. They read several Bible verses together before Mick understood. Finally, they read 1 Peter 2:24:

> Who his own self bare our sins in his own body on the tree, that we, being dead to sins, should live unto righteousness: by whose stripes ye were healed.

When Mick read, "Who Himself bore Mick's sins in his body on the tree, so that Mick would die to sins and live to righteousness, by whose stripes Mick was healed," it hit home. "Wow, He did that for me! I was a bum. I smoked pot, did drugs, didn't give a thought about spiritual things, but He did it for me!"

Wanderer

Mick was done with drugs and the party life, but he was still a wanderer. On his way to Alaska with a friend, he stopped in Port Townsend, Washington. After a disappointing visit with an old girlfriend, he decided to camp out by the sea. At sunset, he went to take a picture from the ledge of a cliff. The ledge

Mick

broke. Mick fell sixty-five feet and rolled another sixty feet. He lay on the beach all night. When he was found, he was flown to a hospital. He had broken his pelvis in three places and had to have a body cast for two months. When he was discharged, his mom and Ivan flew him back to Omaha.

After more travels, service in numerous Christian organizations, and lots of adventure, Mick was brought to another crisis. He had married a fellow missionary whom he had met on a mission trip, but his marriage had failed. In 2020, he was alone in western North Dakota, and he decided to move to Arizona where he could be near his only son. He had everything packed and was ready to go when he completely totaled his car. Not knowing what else to do, he wondered if he should go to Valley City, North Dakota, where Phil and Tammy were living. Less than two days later, Tammy texted him, "Why don't you move to Valley City?"

Mick took this as a nudge from God. He moved to Valley City, and God used it for good. Mick left his checkered past behind him and grew spiritually in fellowship with Phil and Tammy and the Christians in their church.

These confessed that they were strangers and pilgrims on the earth.
—Hebrews 11:13

CHAPTER 9

Kim

Tammy's little sister Kim was a teenager when Tammy embarked on a new life in Christ Jesus. She had experienced a similar childhood to Tammy, but she hadn't processed it. She couldn't see through the darkness and confusion that her sordid upbringing had created, and she wasn't ready to take the same step of faith that Tammy had.

Dark mystery had characterized Kim's life since her birth in 1963. Before she developed language and understanding, she was moved from one abusive mother to another. When she was a toddler, mysterious things happened around the house. Her only companion and friend was blamed for them and severely punished. Kim and Tammy spent all their time in a room with the door closed. A thin piece of tape ensured that they stayed in. Tammy never left, so who caused the vandalism?

Throughout Kim's childhood, her precious sister disappeared at times. Little Kim had no idea where she was. Sometimes she returned after a few hours, but on at least two occasions, she was gone for months. When Tammy was gone, the mysterious damage to furnishings continued. Kim was blamed for it. When Tammy returned, the two girls silently shared their sorrows, but when she was gone, Kim was devastatingly alone.

On the rare occasion that her stepmother, Betty, was gone to visit family, the vandalism and the beatings stopped. Kim was too young to piece the circumstantial evidence together and see the whole picture, but she enjoyed the brief interlude of a normal homelife. She and Tammy were allowed out of their room, and they went to a fun restaurant with their dad. When Betty returned, the torture and isolation resumed. More than once, Kim was beaten until she passed out.

Besides Tammy and, in a limited way, the housekeeper, June, the only friendly face in Kim's life was her Grandpa Cotton. One day, without saying a thing to her, Dad and Grandpa came to the room and packed up Tammy's things. Mystified, Kim watched in horror as her dad took Tammy away. She tried to run after them, but Grandpa held her back. Kim was abandoned. She didn't know where Tammy had gone, but she sensed that she wouldn't be coming back.

With the help of sympathetic neighbors who had been informed by the babysitter of what was going on, Tammy was able to arrange two brief phone calls to Kim. These 30-second calls to the neighbor's house were top-secret. Kim learned nothing about where her sister was. She got to hear Tammy's voice. The girls told each other, "I love you," then little Kim returned to the torture of loneliness at home.

When the housekeeper's mother died, Kim spotted Tammy at the funeral. She tried to run up to her, but again she was held back. Kim was not allowed to see or talk to Tammy.

Losing his children, but not willing to face his own actions or the consequences that naturally proceeded from them, Kim and Tammy's father was tormented inside. In a wild fit of rage and confusion, after Tammy went to live with her mom, Channing tore up the bathroom and shattered the mirror. But he did not deal with his sin. His pain was centered in his own loss, not that which he caused his children. He realized that he couldn't have both Betty and his daughters. He chose Betty.

Betty had systematically removed each of Channing's children from his home and from his life. Kim, the baby, was the last to go. Channing and Betty made their plans to move to Minnesota without her.

Kim's dad asked her if she wanted to live with Tammy. "Wherever Tammy is, I want to be," was Kim's sentiment. She didn't know that her parents planned to move and that she would only see her dad twice a year. She didn't know that she would be largely separated from the Cotton side of the family, and that she wouldn't find out about her grandpa's funeral until months after it happened. And she didn't know that she would be trading an evil stepmother for a crazy mom.

When Channing dropped Kim off at Ivan and Mary's, he pulled up in front of the neighbor's house. Sitting in the car, he gave her a bit of information that her young mind could barely grasp. He told her that Betty was not her mom, and that she was going to be living with her real mother. He didn't take her to the door. She stood in the yard with her jaw on the ground as she watched the car disappear down the road.

Mick and Tammy met Kim outside and took her up to the house. They explained that she should call Mary and Ivan *Mom* and *Dad* and she should tell Mary that she loved her. This was all so confusing to her undeveloped understanding. She didn't care about Betty, but how could she say, "I love you," to someone she didn't know—someone of whose existence, until that moment, she had not even known.

Soon she would learn the full horror of her situation. She went from being an isolated child in an upper-class family to being a roughly-treated servant in an old house in a neglected neighborhood. Tammy taught her to dust and scrub the bathroom. She had a long list of chores to do before she could play. She learned to tiptoe around all day while her mother slept. Day after day involved a new kind of tension. She had her dearly-beloved sister, but all was not well.

At just short of eight years old, Kim was expected to process the revelation that the woman she had called "Mom" was not her mom. An unknown, unpredictable, and unloving woman was her mother. Kim had been torn from one painful situation and thrown into a worse one. At a much younger age than Tammy, she was exposed to the realities of mental illness, alcoholism, drug abuse, and rage. She moved from a home with physical abuse and emotional neglect to one of chaos, emotional abuse, and physical danger. Her mother hated her, and she wasn't shy to say so. She told Kim plainly that she was only in the house because Tammy and Mick wanted her. She did not. Once Kim was in the house, the violence that regularly erupted from Mary was focused primarily at her.

A Refuge

When teen-aged Tammy moved out of Ivan and Mary's house, she remained Kim's lifeline. Phil became like a brother to her. They were the only loving constant in her life. When she could no longer stay at home, Kim took refuge with her sister. Tammy, barely out of her teens herself, had done the necessary paperwork to take over guardianship for Kim and had found them a place to live together—upstairs from Grandma Hamilton.

When the gospel first penetrated Tammy's heart, and she began to change, the confusion of the situation troubled Kim to the core. Darkness and fear gripped her. Tammy wasn't physically leaving, but the Tammy she had always known and leaned on was gone. Phil was angry. He wanted things to stay the same, and Kim sided with him. She was afraid of losing them both.

When Phil changed, too, Kim was glad for her sister's sake, but she still didn't know what to make of it. She loved Tammy dearly. She was thankful for the haven that her sister had given her, but she was a teenager trying to see through an unbelievably dark past and make her own way in the world. The false accusations she had faced as a child made her particularly resistant to subtle condemnation. She wasn't a follower. She pushed back in defiance against subtle pressure to conform. She hung out with Phil and Tammy's new friends and attended the same church that they did, but she maintained a degree of skepticism about their ways and their form of religion. Like Tammy, she adored Grandma Hamilton. Through Grandma's influence, she began to see that many of her religious notions had been wrong, but she didn't open her heart like Tammy had. The pain was too great. It wasn't until a few years later, when she found herself pregnant, that she cried out to God.

Kim had had a boyfriend on and off through high school. Tiring of his games, she got swept off her feet by another. After dating him for only three weeks, Kim became pregnant. The father of her child was not worthy of Kim's adoration. He wasn't ready for responsibility, and he didn't want to be a part of the baby's life, so he and Kim parted ways. Lonely and devastated, and having nowhere else to turn, Kim looked to her sister and the church family for support.

Not Alone

On July 4, 1984, after Wednesday night Bible study, Phil's friend Ken Rempel went for a walk with Kim. The sun was setting in the evening sky as they stood on the sidewalk together. In the middle of a conversation that is now a blur, these words pierced her soul: "Kim, with the Lord in your heart and in your life, no matter where you are, who you are with, or even by yourself, you will never be alone!"

The truth of God's love for her and His abiding presence flooded her soul. Everything changed. She could trust God! She didn't hear angels sing. No light bulbs turned on. No fireworks went off. Her confidence was quiet and subtle, just a whisper, but it was enough for her to finally hear what everyone had been saying for the previous three years and trying to show her in the Bible. She had clarity and peace. The next morning she woke up to sunshine. A weight had been lifted off her chest, and she felt secure. She knew she was not alone. She could not do life alone, and she did not have to.

Kim's first son was born that December. His dad contacted her on Christmas Eve. He expressed a change of heart, and Kim, desperate for the three of them to be a family, allowed him into her life. Unfortunately, she put him ahead of the Lord Jesus. God's word did not get the priority it ought to have had, and Kim suffered for the choice. Her husband was unfaithful. He was in and out of her life many times, and he broke her heart over and over again as she waited for him to return. After three more children and fourteen years on and off, the relationship ended in divorce.

Because of her experience after the Bible study in 1984, Kim never felt as completely alone as she otherwise would have. She hung onto the words that had been spoken to her and believed that Jesus was there for her, waiting for her to return, though she was not serving Him. Having turned to the things of the world and neglected the Lord Jesus, Kim naturally felt unhappy. She was dissatisfied with herself and her life. After her divorce, she had an emotional breakdown and went into a downhill spiral. One bad decision led to another, going deeper and deeper into sin and misery.

Kim had various unsatisfying relationships and three more children within five years. She worked hard to provide good homes for her seven kids, but she neglected their spiritual training and her own spiritual health. As she realized this, she started looking for a church, but it was easy to find excuses not to go. She had been personally wounded at one church, and she feared others would look down on her for the mistakes in her life. Some churches had progressive theology. Some bent the Bible to suit their own will. Some emphasized gaining attendees over upholding the truth. She found it so disappointing that she didn't want to be a part of it. Just when she thought she may have found a church family, something would come up to turn her away. Despite relying more and more on Jesus in her daily life, she dragged her feet about going back to church and getting serious about following Him.

Covid

Then Covid hit. The earthly government overreached its power and promoted fear and isolation. Businesses, churches, entertainments, and even shopping were closed, supposedly for two weeks. The panic and draconian laws lasted much longer. Kim felt like she had been slapped upside the head. The measures which the government enforced gave her time alone to think, and she turned it into an opportunity for prayer. She had many conversations with God, asking for guidance. She prayed aloud and thanked Him for everything, both the good and the bad in her life. She started earnestly looking for a church, and she spent a lot of time at online church services. Most of them, unfortunately, included disappointing, progressive trappings.

Kim remembered the prophetic teaching that she had heard from Grandma Hamilton and Phil back in the eighties. The things that they had talked about then were coming to pass. She watched the news, saw the evil all around, and knew the end was coming. It was a wake-up call to get back on track with the Lord. She sobbed her heart out to God, asking for forgiveness from the depths of her soul, recognizing His worthiness to have control of everything in her life.

Kim texted a friend whom she knew to be a Christian and got connected with her church, Westside Church in Omaha, which she has made her home church. She is actively living for Christ and looking for His return. By His grace, she is trying to grow closer to Him and truer to His word. She has turned her eyes off the troubles of this world. She no longer seeks for fulfillment from men. The Lord Jesus is her hope and her salvation. She is looking forward to a rich, eternal life with Christ. She has no fear of illness or death, and she has determined not to spread fear by conforming to unnecessary regulations. Her only concern is for her kids, other family members, and friends who do not know the Lord and have no desire to open their hearts to Him.

Over the years, Satan wormed his way into her life and into many of her family members, corrupting them with false beliefs and false comfort. It saddens her to see it, though she knows the Bible foretold that this would happen, particularly in the last days.

Choosing to forgive is difficult. For so many years, Kim took a worldly path, accumulating more sorrow and confusion. She prefers not to dig through it or think about all she has been through. She rests her heart in God's hands and in His plan, no longer being controlled by the devil's deception.

For he hath said, I will never leave thee, nor forsake thee.
—Hebrews 13:5

CHAPTER 10

Relationships Redeemed

When Tammy trusted Christ with her life, she didn't know what would happen to her relationship with Phil. She committed the matter to God, believing that He would give her what was best. He did. Phil and Tammy were saved in February, 1981, twelve days apart. They planned to get married in May.

Tammy wanted her dad to walk her down the aisle at the wedding. He wrote her a letter, saying he would do so only if she apologized to Betty. Tammy was livid with rage. "Me apologize?!" Betty was the one who ought to apologize to her, and her dad had to know it!

Tammy fumed over her dad's unreasonable request. She could have nursed her resentment and alienated her father completely. Instead, she let God work a miracle in her heart. She poured over God's word, reading it on the bus during her daily trips to and from work. One day she read:

> Recompense to no man evil for evil. Provide things honest in the sight of all men. If it be possible, as much as lieth in you, live peaceably with all men. Dearly beloved, avenge not yourselves, but rather give place unto wrath: for it is written, Vengeance is mine; I will repay, saith the Lord. Therefore if thine enemy hunger,

feed him; if he thirst, give him drink: for in so doing thou shalt heap coals of fire on his head. Be not overcome of evil, but overcome evil with good (Rom. 12:17-21).

As she read, she believed. The Spirit of God took away the bitterness of her heart. In a moment, she was completely freed of the hatred for her stepmother that had characterized her past. She looked to God for grace and prayed for help to write a letter. She couldn't apologize for things she hadn't done. She hadn't gouged furniture or disobeyed her parents, but she had harbored deep resentment towards Betty. She wrote to Betty, apologizing for her bad attitude and admitting that she had been angry and bitter towards her. This apology was accepted. Without any repentance or acknowledgement of the wrong done to her by her stepmother, the relationship was redeemed.

Wedding

Channing Cotton walked his daughter down the aisle at her wedding, May 9, 1981. Bill Fear performed the ceremony at the Keystone Bible Chapel. Mary Fear helped with the wedding arrangements.

At the ceremony, Aunt Cheryl stepped out in front of Tammy to snap a picture as she and her dad were walking down the aisle. Tammy hadn't seen Cheryl since the day of her missed band concert in 1970. She almost stopped the wedding to run over and hug her, but she controlled herself and waited until after the ceremony.

The following November, all the Cottons gathered at Aunt Cheryl's farm. Channing, Betty, Mick, Kim, and Phil and Tammy were all there. Despite the pain and the past, they were all together. Tammy had not seen Betty or her daughters since she had left for her mom's house ten years earlier. She had barely seen her father. By God's grace, she was able to overcome all ill feelings toward her step family and establish normal relationships with them. She was able even to show love to Julie without mentioning the horrible scenes that had transpired in her youth.

After Tammy's first child was born, she and Phil went to her father's lake house in Minnesota. Though a different structure in a different state, everything about it reminded Tammy of the home she had grown up in. It had dark walls with similar adornments and the exact same furnishings.

When Tammy laid her baby down to change his diaper, she noticed a large scratch on the dresser. A moment of panic overtook her. Had she done something to it? No, she quickly realized. It was an old scratch, one that Betty had inflicted herself and punished Tammy for. Why hadn't she gotten rid of the damaged furniture? The evidence of Tammy's childhood abuse was disturbing in the extreme. Everywhere Tammy looked, memories screamed at her and reopened deeply buried wounds. How did it not have a similar effect on Betty? So hardened and so blind was her stepmother that she could look on the marks of her own wickedness and not see them at all.

Muskies

Channing and Betty lived in a big log home on Leech Lake. The exterior needed to be stained and sealed every four years. Not being in the best of health, Channing tried to do one side a year. Even so, it was a challenge for him. Phil offered to help. He told his father-in-law to rent a sprayer. "You and I can knock it out in two days!"

Betty didn't think it could be done. Tammy helped cover the windows, and the guys sprayed the house in two long days. Betty was thrilled. She packed the guys a lunch and sent them out fishing. Her husband fished every day, but not always with the blessing he got that day.

Musky are called the fish of ten thousand casts. Channing had caught plenty of them. His first summer at his lake home, he caught 108. Soon after, he worked with the DNR to track the spawning beds on Leech Lake. Channing and a friend who worked for the DNR caught the fish. Then "Doc" Cotton performed a procedure on them, putting in a tracking device. By this means, the DNR could track where the muskies were breeding and protect them from the developers who were coming in to create resorts along the lake shore.

Phil had heard about Doc years earlier. Back then, he had not taken the time to wait for the famous fisherman's advice. Now he was Doc's son-in-law. Despite the man's shortcomings as a dad, Phil honored him as his wife's father, and he counted it an honor to go fishing with him. As they were getting off the lake, Phil pulled in a huge musky. It still graces the wall of his study.

Betty

When Betty got sick in the late eighties, the doctors in Minnesota and North Dakota were not able to determine what was wrong. Finally, Betty went to Omaha. There she was diagnosed with pancreatic cancer and admitted to the hospital. She had little chance of living very long.

On various occasions, Tammy and Phil had told her about her need for Christ, but so far Betty had been unresponsive. Now they were praying for another chance. Tammy was in a waiting room with other family members when an agitated nurse entered and asked, "Who is Tammy?"

Tammy said, "I am."

"She's screaming for you. You must come upstairs," said the nurse urgently.

Tammy went into the room and began to talk to Betty about the Lord Jesus. Betty went ballistic, thrashing in her bed. The nurse medicated her, and a drug-induced calm subdued her.

Betty's birthday was coming up. She wanted to go home to Minnesota for her birthday. Her medical staff allowed her two weeks, then she was to return for more treatment.

The day she was supposed to return to Nebraska, Betty said to her husband, "You can carry me from the bedroom to the bathroom. From the bathroom to the living room. From the living room to the kitchen. Why can't you carry me to heaven?"

"I'm not going back to Nebraska," she said. Then she laid her head on Channing's chest and died. It was April 1989.

Mary and Ivan

Tammy saw her responsibility to honor her parents, regardless of what they were or what they had done. The promise "that it may be well with you," was for her on the condition of giving honor to her parents, but there was no condition on the parents. Though they had wronged her, Tammy wanted to honor them for Christ's sake. It hasn't been easy, but God gave her the strength she needed to honor all of them for their position as her parents.

> Honor thy father and mother; (which is the first commandment with promise;) That it may be well with thee, and thou mayest live long on the earth (Eph. 6:2-3).

From the beginning of their marriage, Phil and Tammy reached out to Mary and Ivan and spent time with them as a family. When they had children, they brought the kids over to their grandparents' house.

Ivan had quit drinking. His employer had required him to go through treatment in order to keep his job. He complied, and took up coffee instead of Falstaff.

Three or four years after Tammy came to Christ, her mother, Mary, attended Bible study with her. She made a profession of faith, saying, "You know I'm a sinner." Later she called Tammy and asked for forgiveness, admitting that she had been a terrible mother. She was the only one of Tammy's parents to confess any fault to her. Hearing this confession of sin was a great help to Tammy, and she was able to release her anger toward her mother.

Mary's warped perception of reality made her difficult to be around, even after she had admitted her failure as a mother. There were times when Tammy, for the sake of her own sanity, had to back away, rather than try to deal with her mother's demented way of thinking. One of these was when Mick fell off a cliff and was lying in a Washington hospital in a coma. Tammy found out about it when a local news reporter called and asked her how he was doing. Knowing that her mom would be asleep, Tammy called her dad, "Do you know about Mick?" He didn't. Channing called the hospital and then flew out to Washington to be with Mick while he recovered.

Mary had been informed about Mick's accident two days prior, but she had not contacted Tammy or any other family members. When Tammy talked to her later, she was angry. "Who do you think you are getting involved?" Mary complained and hung up on Tammy.

On August 24, 1989, Tammy got a call from Ivan. Mary was having a heart procedure done. She had not wanted Ivan to tell the girls, and they had not known that she had been seeing a doctor for heart issues. At the last minute, Ivan felt compelled to tell them about the angiogram. Tammy and Kim found babysitters for their children and went to the hospital. They sat with Ivan in the waiting room outside Xray. Fifteen minutes after they arrived, they heard the intercom flash Code Blue. An hour later, a staff member came and asked them to the quiet room. Kim and Tammy wondered what was up, but they had not the slightest suspicion that she may have died. She had tried to take her own life many times and had never succeeded.

The hospital staff said, "I'm sorry we could not revive her."

Tammy and Kim looked at each other. They didn't believe it. "No way." "She doesn't die," they said. "She's had last rites so many times!"

"Do you want to see her?"

The staff escorted them to the exam room. They saw her dead body on the exam table. They had seen her in a similar state many times before. They had to touch her to know for sure that she was dead. She couldn't wreak havoc in their lives anymore.

No tears were shed.

Ivan lived for another twelve years. Phil and Tammy and the kids continued a cordial relationship with him throughout his life, but he never wanted to talk about spiritual matters. He went to the coffee shop daily and visited with the waitresses. He was a pleasant person, and everyone loved him. He didn't see himself as a sinner, and he didn't need a Savior. He died of cancer in 2002.

Israel, put your hope in the Lord, for with the Lord is unfailing love and with him is full redemption. —Psalm 130:7 NIV

CHAPTER 11

Resolution

Abuse clings to a victim, and its rippling effect is serious. Tammy had expected that, at some point, her past would catch up with her and affect her parenting. Nonetheless, she was startled when it happened. One day while sweeping the kitchen, she noticed her young son picking on his little sister. In a gut response that she couldn't control, she beat him with the broom in her hand.

This was not how she wanted to treat her children! She intended to break the cycle of abuse! What was happening? She called Mary Fear.

Mary gave Tammy some books that contained a mixture of modern psychology and solid, biblical truth.[1] God used them to help Tammy understand herself and to look past the humans who had hurt her. She began to see that the pain she had harbored had damaged her perception of God. She was still harboring resentment towards Him for the childhood she had experienced.

Tammy had trusted God for salvation and had felt the initial joy of knowing that He cared for her. God's goodness had penetrated her heart and changed her completely. He had instantly removed her hatred for her stepfamily, but that was not all the work that needed to be done. The layers of pain had not gone away.

The death of both her mothers in 1989 caused the pain of Tammy's childhood to resurface. She had always harbored a futile hope that she could have a normal relationship with her birth mother. Death intervened with finality. She had to face that it was never going to be better than it was.

Betty's death dragged up deeply buried wrong attitudes. Tammy had always focused the pain of her earlier childhood towards Betty. Now she was gone. She no longer stood between Tammy and her father. Subconsciously, Tammy had assumed that with Betty gone, her relationship with her dad would improve. He would become the father that she had always wanted.

Tammy loved, and nearly idolized, her father. She blamed Betty for all her troubles. With Betty as a scapegoat, she had been defending and justifying her father for his part in her sorrows. Since her dad was effectually untouchable, Tammy's lingering pain and anger were imperceptibly directed towards God. He had allowed her painful childhood, and she viewed Him as a silent partner in the abuse.

Healing

As Tammy's daughter got older and closer to the age that Tammy had been when she was abused, watching her brought back memories of her own bitter childhood. Her desire to protect her little girl was intertwined with long-suppressed pain. The ugliness that had been buried deep inside her hadn't been dealt with, and it started leaking out. She wasn't experiencing the peaceful home that she had wanted. Instead, she was easily angered with Phil, as well as with her son.

One day in the fall, 1989, Tammy, as she was homeschooling, read a children's story to the kids about Caleb and Joshua, who were sent to spy out the land of Canaan. They reported that the land was beautiful with lots of fruit. There were giants, too, but Caleb and Joshua trusted the Lord. As she read,

Resolution

God spoke to her heart, "Don't be afraid. You need to deal with your giants." She didn't want to revisit and reopen her old wounds, but she knew she had to. She decided to get Christian counseling, as had been recommended in the books she had been reading.

Tammy told the counselor, "I see pieces of the puzzle, but I don't know how to put it all together."

The counselor listened and prayed with her. She helped Tammy to distinguish between her earthly and her heavenly Father. She told Tammy, "You need to direct your anger where it belongs. Your father is a sinner. God is not. You can't hold God responsible for your father's actions."

Tammy didn't intend to be in counseling for long. She wanted the counselor to help her get victory. Then she intended to leave her problems and her therapy behind. God honored her desire. She had been in counseling about two months when the opportunity came for her to get beyond the need of it.

The holidays were approaching. As a reaction to the painful Christmases of her own childhood, Tammy went out of her way to make sure Christmas was special for her children. Instead of quarreling, drunkenness, broken furniture, and blood, she coveted a time of peace and celebration, and she included extended family as much as possible. Her dad joined her and Phil every other year, spending the off years with Betty's family.

This year, it was Tammy's turn to host her dad. Instead of following the usual schedule, Channing decided to spend Christmas with Betty's daughters. Already struggling with her past, Tammy was deeply hurt. She was infuriated that even with Betty gone, her father's allegiance was still with Betty's family over her.

The stepsister Channing was staying with had a family emergency on her husband's side. Consequently, Channing had nowhere left to stay. He called and asked Tammy if he could go to her place after all.

Tammy exploded. "Are you kidding? I'm second fiddle, and you want to come see me now? No way!"

Phil intervened. He told Tammy, "You need to take this opportunity." He told Channing to come over and have a long talk with his daughter.

Tammy called her counselor. The Christian mentor gently said to her, "Remember the giants in the land? With the Lord's help, we can overcome them." Tammy knew it was time to face her giants. She didn't want to. She was strained emotionally, and she would have rather hidden from the pain. But she knew this was the way that she needed to take to get victory in her life.

> No temptation has overtaken you except such as is common to man; but God is faithful, who will not allow you to be tempted beyond what you are able, but with the temptation will also make the way of escape, that you may be able to bear it (1 Cor. 10:13 NKJV).

Tammy agreed to allow her dad to come over to the house, not to spend the night and celebrate the holidays, but to talk.

"Did you find the diamond bracelet?" was Tammy's question when they sat down together.

Channing hung his head.

"You did, didn't you! It wasn't gone. Did you really believe I did those things?"

"I was caught between two loves," he said. "You may find this hard to believe, but I tried to protect you."

"You did a horrible job of it," Tammy responded. "You know, you taught me a lot. You taught me what not to do. I didn't repeat any of it."

Channing never admitted his guilt. He never repented or said I'm sorry. So absent was he in Tammy's childhood that he didn't even remember most of the things she brought up. On the other hand, he didn't challenge her interpretation. He allowed her to talk. Tammy let loose the pent-up hurts of all the years. They talked for six or seven hours.

Tammy forgave her dad.

Channing didn't acknowledge his guilt, but Tammy did. She admitted that he was the cause of her pain, not God. There was healing in moving her expectations for love and affection off a fellow mortal and placing them on God. Her faith was deepened in its core aspect: Trusting that God is good despite the wickedness He allows on the earth.

Mercy

In our fallen world, God allows man to have free will. It is only of His mercy that we are not consumed (Lam. 3:22). God grieves over the pain that mortals inflict on one another. The day is coming when He will return to earth and stop all the sorrow and pain. When He does, He will do a thorough work.

> When the Lord Jesus shall be revealed from heaven with his mighty angels, in flaming fire taking vengeance on them that know not God, and that obey not the gospel of our Lord Jesus Christ (2 Thess. 1:7-8).

Meanwhile, He calls sinners to repentance and requires us to forgive one another, even as He has forgiven us (Eph. 4:32).

Need of Grace

The way of grace is better than wishing for what's fair;
One servant to another is foolish to compare.
The grace of God, unmeasured, fills far too great a span
For us to see a difference in any given man.

If one receives a blessing another doesn't get,
He's still to God a debtor; there's no excuse to fret.
It's only of God's mercies that we are not consumed;
Man's efforts to be righteous in every case are doomed.

The depths to which we've fallen appear to us diverse;
Men seem, from our perspective, some better and some worse,
But none are fit for heaven nor earn themselves a place,
For all fall short of glory, and all have need of grace.

Channing

The seven-hour long talk with her dad brought Tammy resolution. Imperfect though the outcome was, it enabled her to move forward. The pain was not gone, but it was no longer boiling inside her. It no longer interfered with her relationship with God, and it no longer burst out in irrational behavior toward Phil or her children.

Now that she had dismissed subconscious expectations from her dad and was no longer looking for him to be what she had always hoped and wanted, she could bask in her adoption by God. With steadfast assurance that God loved her, she could accept her dad as a flawed human being like herself and share the love of God with him.

Phil and Tammy visited Channing in Minnesota every couple years. He appreciated, respected, and loved Phil. He loved spending time with the grandchildren and taking his son-in-law fishing. The kids enjoyed their grandpa and the visits to the lake.

Phil and Tammy tried to speak to Channing about the claims of Christ on his life. He wouldn't hear it. He was consumed with a love for this world. He enjoyed the good things of life and didn't seem to feel his need to do anything about the next one.

Channing had had several heart attacks while still a young man. As he aged, he developed diabetes and kidney disease. When he neared death, Phil and Tammy made more frequent trips to visit him, sometimes dropping everything and driving through the night when he called for them. He seemed to soften, and he allowed Phil to talk to him about God and the scientific aspects of creation.

Due to complications with his spleen, Channing was scheduled for a surgery to have it removed. There was a high risk that he would die on the operating table. Phil and Tammy accompanied him to the hospital. The day before his surgery, his bloodwork was surprisingly normal. The surgeon said to him, "Mayo Clinic would love for me to do surgery on you. They would make a lot of money off you, but I'm not prepared to throw snake eyes. I have two people die on me a year, and I don't want you to be one of them tomorrow. I'm here to tell you to pack your bags and go home." Channing was cured of all issues with his spleen.

After this event, Channing had a stroke which limited his mobility. He fell off his dock and wounded his leg. Because of his diabetes, the leg became infected and needed to be amputated.

Channing was on dialysis. His kidney doctor said to him, "You can end all this. We are keeping you alive. You don't have to keep doing dialysis." Channing chose to quit the dialysis, expecting to die within twenty-four to forty-eight hours. He lived ten days.

During those ten days, family members took turns watching over Channing at his bedside. While Phil and Tammy were out for dinner, Kim and some of the other family members were gathered around his bed. They heard the death rattle in his breathing, and they knew he would be going soon. They watched as he took a long inhale. He then exhaled and was gone.

"NO! NO!" Channing woke up screaming and rocking back and forth in bed. The family was frightened, and a nurse anesthetized him.

Phil and Tammy walked into the room and noticed the wide-eyed fear in the faces of the people around Channing's bed. Kim said, "He died. I know he died. You should have seen it."

The others left, and Phil and Tammy took their turn to watch over the bed. The Christian nurse told Tammy, "He can hear everything you're saying. Tell him what you want him to hear."

"Dad, just touch the hem of His garment," Tammy said. She then preached verse after verse about the goodness of God to receive sinners. He was calm, and he remained calm until he died three days later.

A friend of Channing's approached Tammy after his funeral. He had been a drinking buddy, but he had turned his life over to Christ a few years before. During Channing's last years, this friend had spoken to him about Christ and the gospel. He told Tammy that after Channing's stroke, he had learned to quote Psalm 23, a fact that is particularly striking since the stroke had robbed him of his ability to speak more than one or two syllables at a time.

Perhaps Channing did, in his dying moments, finally admit his need of a savior. When she gets to heaven, after falling at the feet of the Lord Jesus, the first person Tammy will look for will be her dad.

Scars

Full healing will come only in the resurrection. Until then, scars remain. Memories are not erased. As Vietnamese war survivor Kim Phuc Phan Thi says, "Once we see something, we cannot unsee it. Once we hear something, we cannot unhear it. Once we live something, we cannot unlive it."[2] Even when the painful things in life are working for our good, the residue of bad experiences still exists.

The events of life repeatedly bring to Tammy's recollection intense pain and disturbing emotions. For example, Tammy and Phil go into the jails to minister to inmates. When Tammy hears the doors lock behind her, the realization that she is not at liberty to freely use the bathroom can cause moments of panic in which she is tortured with the horror of being confined to her room as a child. Every day she must choose to focus on the Lord Jesus Christ and His Word. She throws herself into His work and looks forward to His return when He will wash away all tears. Until then, she must be vigilant in the battle to maintain a cheerful attitude. She must cast down the strongholds of the devil and block his fiery darts.

When memories tempt Tammy to negative thoughts about God, she vents her anger back to her dad, and asks God to take it away. She clings to the verse, "vengeance is mine, saith the Lord" (Rom. 12:19).

And I am sure of this, that he who began a good work in you will bring it to completion at the day of Jesus Christ.
—Philippians 1:6 ESV

CHAPTER 12

New Life

As soon as Phil and Tammy let the Lord Jesus shine His light into their lives, they got involved in Grandma's church, Keystone Bible Chapel. They were baptized there two or three weeks after making a profession of faith. Tammy was elated to *bury the dead man*, and rise in newness of life. Phil was happy to do whatever the Lord required.

At church, Tammy listened intently to the preaching, but she didn't always understand the meaning of what was being spoken. One Sunday shortly after she first started going to the chapel, the preacher talked about presenting our first fruits to the Lord, meaning that we give Him our top priority and give Him our best gifts. Eager to give back to the Lord who had loved her, she took the message literally. The next Sunday she prepared a large basket of fresh fruit. When Phil saw it, he asked what it was for.

"Weren't you listening? They told us to bring fruit with us."

Phil figured he missed that part. When they arrived at the door of the chapel, the preacher asked why she had brought the basket of fruit.

"Last week you told us to bring fruit!"

"Oh, honey, that's precious!"

Tammy was embarrassed, but the saints at the chapel saw the fruit of the Spirit in her actions.

Instead of going out and getting drunk with their group of friends, Phil and Tammy's whole life revolved around the things of God. They got together with their friends to talk about the Bible and *The Late, Great Planet Earth* by Hal Lindsey.

Public Testimony

With the help of Bill and Mary Fear, Phil and Tammy planned a wedding at the Keystone Bible Chapel. They decided that it would be a good time to let their family know about the change in their lives. Phil and Tammy each wrote out the personal testimony of how the Lord Jesus had changed them for eternity.

Phil's stomach was tied in knots. He was worried about giving his testimony at the wedding, so had come home early from the rehearsal dinner to rest in his upstairs room. The devil tormented him all through the night. On the day of the wedding, Phil called Grandma and told her he couldn't go through with his intention. "I'm scared to death. I can't do it."

Grandma said, "The Lord will understand, Phil." Then she added, "Will you read me a passage?" She turned him to 2 Corinthians 12:9:

> My grace is sufficient for thee: for my strength is made perfect in weakness. Most gladly therefore will I rather glory in my infirmities, that the power of Christ may rest upon me.

"I have a question," she continued. "Can you supply the weakness?"

"Grandma, that's all I've got."

"You get on your knees and tell God that."

Phil got on his knees and got up again with a new resolve. He didn't get a superman suit, but he did get peace in his heart that God would show up and give him the strength he needed to bear public testimony to His grace and goodness towards him, a weak sinner.

Phil was getting married. Rather than thinking about his wife, his marriage, or his future, he was shaking in his boots with fear over bearing testimony for Christ. The upside, however, of speaking about the Lord Jesus at his wedding was twofold. One, it set a precedence for a life of sharing the gospel and putting Christ Jesus first in his life, a choice that has borne much fruit for eternity over the years. Two, Phil's brother Kelly, who was the best man at the wedding, received eternal salvation, largely on account of that testimony.

The officiant, Bill Fear gave a gospel message, then said, "Phil and Tammy have something they desire to tell you, something that's so important to them that they want to tell you about it."

The beautiful bride went first. In simple, heart-felt language, she told how God had transformed her.

Kelly Kleymann

Kelly had seen a change in his brother Joe. Then Phil and Tammy had gotten the new religion. He wasn't sure what to make of it. As Phil's best man, he was standing with the wedding party during the ceremony. He was taken aback when Tammy began to give her testimony. Oh, no! It dawned on him that Phil would be doing the same thing. He looked over at his younger brother. Sweat was forming on his brow, and he looked weak. When he opened his mouth, the first sounds were squeaks. Then Phil straightened up and told his story.

Kelly feared there would be a reaction, but he wondered why people would be upset about faith in Christ. He had seen a lifestyle change in two brothers and a few friends. He was happy for them to get away from the self-destructive life they had been leading. Who are the better Christians? The ones angry with people who have stopped drinking and smoking dope? Or the ones talking about Jesus and giving out Bibles?

Phil had given Kelly a Bible as his gift for participating in the wedding. Kelly decided to read it. One Sunday afternoon while swimming at a little lake, Phil talked further to Kelly about faith in Christ. He asked if Kelly was reading his Bible. Kelly said he was, but he wasn't sure where to read.

"Read John's gospel," Phil suggested.

Kelly had some time before a hockey game, so he read the book of John. When he got to the crucifixion, it made him mad. "Why didn't Jesus smoke them all?" he thought.

As he drove to the hockey arena, he thought about Jesus on the cross and realized, "Jesus allowed it, endured it for me!" In front of him on the road were three guys on motorcycles. As he watched them, he thought, "Kelly, that's who you used to be, laughing and having a good time, and not caring about what you just read. That's not who you are anymore."

Kelly pulled off the road and cried. He watched the bikers disappear over the horizon. He knew that Christ had died for him, and his life would never be the same. He got saved on the shoulder of that road and went to hockey practice a new man.

At the next Bible study, Kelly was smiling like the cat that got the canary. A woman noticed his smile and asked, "What are you grinning about?"

"What do you think I'm smiling about?" Kelly said. "I got saved this week."

Ten years later, another of the Kleymann boys experienced true freedom through the gospel of Christ.

Tim Kleymann

Growing up in a religious home, Phil's younger brother, Tim, viewed himself as a privileged member of the one true religion. His baptism and church membership provided him with a golden ticket to heaven. He believed in God but had no interest in spiritual matters, and he thought church was boring. He felt he was a good person, but when he looks back, he is ashamed of so many of the things he did. Starting in the seventh grade, he obtained and consumed large quantities of alcohol, wholly ignorant of the spiritual battle he was losing.

One night in 1981, Tim went to a party where consumption of alcohol was the main event. His brother Joe wasn't drinking like everyone else. He said he had found something better. He gave Tim a Bible for Christmas. When Tim got around to reading it, he started with Revelation. "Wow, that was some weird, wild stuff!" he thought.

Kelly, Joe, and Phil started talking about stories in the Bible at family gatherings, and Tim listened from a distance. He found it interesting and engaging. They seemed excited about it. He was amazed when Phil talked about all the prophecy that had been written about Jesus. The Old Testament prophet, Micah had foretold the Savior would be born in Bethlehem seven hundred years before Jesus was even born.

One night in November, 1992, after a family gathering, Phil and Tim stayed up late, sitting by the fire. Phil talked about Passover and explained how the blood of an innocent lamb had saved the Israelites through their obedience and faith. Now, through the shed blood of Jesus on the cross, He became the perfect sacrificial lamb for us. Tim says:

> It was the most impelling story I have ever heard. That was the spark that started me on my journey to read the Bible and detour from the broad way of the world that I had been traveling. I was walking in darkness and felt somewhat like Saul when the scales fell from his eyes.
>
> I feel so blessed today to be walking with Jesus and to know my wife and three kids are walking in the truth as well. Today, I'm serving as an elder at our church, I'm involved with the Gideons ministry, and I teach fourth to sixth grade Sunday school alongside my wonderful wife of thirty-five years.

It's so comforting to know God loves us so deeply. What would life be like without the greatest hope and joy we have of knowing we will be with Christ one day soon? I'm grateful to my brothers for guiding me into the saving grace of Jesus Christ and the personal relationship I now have with Him.

Grandma's Influence

Phil and Tammy lived upstairs from Grandma for five years. They spent a lot of time with her, learning about the Word and ways of God. They took meals together, and Tammy learned some of her cooking secrets. At Grandma's suggestion, Tammy took up the habit of reading a chapter out of Proverbs every day. She also learned from Grandma about being a Christian wife and mother.

As a young couple, Phil and Tammy had their share of marriage troubles. Coming from a background with divorced parents, the "cut and run" philosophy was part of Tammy's default stress response. More than once in a heated argument, she said, "I'm leaving!" Phil's response was one he had heard from Baptist preacher, Adrian Rogers, "Well, if you're leaving, I'm going with you."

One time after an argument, Tammy packed the kids in the car, planning to go to Minnesota to spend a week with her dad. She didn't even get out of town. She looked in her rearview mirror and saw her kids. She remembered how she had wanted to train her children for Christ and give them a different upbringing than she had had. "This is not right," she told herself. She turned around and went home.

Sunday mornings seemed to be a prime time for arguments. Heated tempers never kept Phil and Tammy from going to church, however. They knew they needed to be there. Often, their anger cooled while they sat quietly together. One or the other of them would reach over and grasp the other's hand.

One time, Phil went fishing on a Saturday night. Tammy was furious. "Do you know what time it is?" she demanded when Phil got home in the wee hours of the morning. She was thinking about the struggle of getting everyone out of bed and ready in time for church the next day.

"Hey, the fishing was so good, I caught two 20-pound catfish," Phil said pleasantly as he dropped his fish on the kitchen floor.

"Two! You were out all night and only caught two fish!" Tammy retorted, as angry as ever. There was no satisfying resolution, but Tammy submitted to her lot as a fisherman's wife, and eventually her anger cooled.

Grandma encouraged hospitality. She told Tammy, "Whatever you have, give it to the Lord." Phil and Tammy often had people over to talk about the things of God. Though they had only a card table, they invited visiting preachers over for meals.

When Grandma had someone over to talk about the things of God, she invited Phil and Tammy down to observe while she opened the Word of God. "Never forget, you are just a page turner," she told them. "Make the Word of God personal and pray for the Spirit of God to show up." She never wanted someone to be pressured into making a profession of salvation because of her. It had to be of God.

Above all, Grandma prayed.

After Phil had been saved a short time, he felt like he was going to set the world on fire and do great things for God. His old friend Rick, another truck driver, and Phil were scheduled to drive empty semi-trailers to Hope, Arkansas. From there, they would wait for a truck coming up from the south and get a ride back to Omaha. Phil figured this was a great opportunity to talk to Rick and the other guy about the gospel.

The shooting of Ronald Reagan on March 30, 1981 was on the news. It set a solemn tone on that hot day in Hope, Arkansas. The only place the truck drivers could get out of the heat was a

New Life

tavern. Phil accompanied his buddies inside. He told himself he wasn't going to drink. They set a cold beer in front of him, and he took it. Then he had a second and a third. Before he knew it, he was as drunk as the other two—and feeling sick with remorse.

When the truck came to pick the guys up, Phil climbed into the back to sleep off his hangover. He awoke to the truck pitching and reeling. He heard Rick calling, "Ohhh." He pulled the curtain open and saw him holding on to the dash. The toothless hillbilly who was driving through the Arkansas mountains was doing his best to jostle them. Laughing, he said, "What's wrong with you flatlanders? You scared?"

Yes, Phil was scared. He had the weight of the world on his back because he had failed God. He had gotten drunk, and he had failed to be a witness. He thought certainly that they would crash. "Everybody's going to be killed," he imagined, "and it'll be my fault." He felt like Jonah on the stormy sea. He wanted to tell the others, "Throw me out! I'm the reason for this trouble."

They didn't crash, and they didn't die, but Phil lost his joy in the Lord. He was a miserable wretch. Tammy couldn't understand what was wrong.

Grandma knew, and she prayed. She didn't know the details, but she knew that something had happened and that Phil had to deal with God about it on his own. After a few days, he drove out into the country at night. Under the stars, he broke down in tears, confessing his sin to God and asking for restored fellowship. It was granted, of course, and Phil came through stronger in faith, though less confident in his own ability to stand.

One day, when Phil was making deliveries in Omaha, Grandma got a sudden urge to pray for him, though she didn't know why. He was hauling a load of turkeys to a grocery store for Thanksgiving. He turned off the interstate in a run-down tractor-trailer, heading toward 90th and Dodge. As he moved downhill towards this busy intersection with forty thousand pounds of boxed turkeys, he realized that his brakes were out.

He had the choice of continuing to the intersection, where he would certainly hit someone, or turning onto the library lawn. Seeing people everywhere, some running from the bus stop, he chose the library. He went over the curb and sank into the soft ground, eventually slowing to a stop. No one was hurt.

When he came home that night, Grandma asked him how his day was. At the exact hour that he was careening towards the intersection, Grandma was earnestly praying, "Lord, Phil needs you, help him."

Soaps

Tammy had watched soap operas as a teenager and young adult. For many years she worked too much to have time for them. When her first child was born, she stayed home with him. She wasn't used to the quiet and wanted noise in the background. Without thinking much about it, she turned the TV to the daytime soap operas. She soon realized this was not profitable for her spiritual well-being, but it wasn't easy to quit. In her Bible reading, she came upon Genesis 4:7 in the Amplified Bible:

> If you do well [believing Me and doing what is acceptable and pleasing to Me], will you not be accepted? And if you do not do well [but ignore My instruction], sin crouches at your door; its desire is for you [to overpower you], but you must master it."

Tammy knew she was not doing well, and she had to master her sin. She wrote out the verse and taped it to the on/off switch on her TV. It worked. She put vinyl Christian records on her stereo to listen to instead of daytime television programming.

God's Provision

Prior to his conversion, Phil had had a traffic accident in Omaha. He took responsibility for the accident, but the person whom he had hit was racking up needless hospital bills on the insurance company. Phil was facing a ten-thousand-dollar lawsuit. Phil and Tammy had nowhere near that much money. Tammy asked a lawyer she knew about dealing with the insurance company, wondering if there was any hope for them or if they would have to file for bankruptcy. He told her plainly the insurance company would not budge. She and Phil took their troubles to the church prayer meeting. There, one of the saints read:

> Be anxious for nothing, but in everything by prayer and supplication, with thanksgiving, let your requests be made known to God; and the peace of God, which surpasses all understanding, will guard your hearts and minds through Christ Jesus (Phil. 4:6-7 NKJV).

Phil took the verse to heart and trusted the Lord with the situation. The following day the insurance company called him to the office. He told them he could pay $100 a week until the full amount was paid off.

"No, that won't work for us. How much can you come up with in one lump sum?"

"By the end of the week, $1,000."

They took it. Tammy's lawyer friend plopped into a chair in disbelief when she told him about it. "That's a miracle," he said.

Living on Phil's income while Tammy stayed home with the kids wasn't easy. One Tuesday night, Tammy went to the freezer and pulled out the last bit of meat. She showed Phil the chicken. She said, "I know what's for dinner tonight. I don't know what's for dinner tomorrow."

Pay day was a few days away. Phil and Tammy's son, Josh, was turning seven soon. Having a cake and a party for him was simply out of the question.

Tammy made the chicken stretch for two meals. They had it again on Wednesday, then went to prayer meeting. When they walked into the chapel's kitchen, there on the counter was a bag with their name on it. It was filled with groceries. Included among much needed items were a box cake and frosting. Josh could have a birthday cake after all! Tammy hadn't told anyone how needy they were. She hadn't even prayed for these things, but God knew she needed them and heard her heart.

Weeks later, as St. Patrick's Day approached, Tammy grumbled to her neighbor that she and Phil couldn't afford to buy corned beef. Within an hour of her complaint, the Lord rebuked her with an over-abundant provision that reminded Phil of the quails that God sent to the grumbling Israelites.

Before Tammy had complained to her friend, a Christian butcher on Phil's truck route had approached him and asked, "Do you like corned beef?"

"Ah, it's OK. I'm not crazy about it," said Phil, "but my wife loves it."

The friend brought out at least twenty pounds of corned beef that was near to the expiration date. "It's perfectly OK," he said, "but I can't sell it."

Phil put the corned beef in the back of his refrigerated truck and brought it home. He stepped into the neighbor's house where Tammy was and threw the twenty-pound bag on the table. "This is for you," he told Tammy. She looked inside. Two large bags of corned beef tips! Tammy and her friend looked at each other in awe. They didn't say a word, but they both enjoyed the corned beef for many meals to come.

Another time when the family was in financial straits, Phil considered asking the neighbor for money that was owed to him. No, he quickly decided not to do it. He had been preaching to this guy. He didn't want anything to get between them. He decided instead to pray. "Lord, you know our needs. You know the money that Doug owes me would be really helpful right now, but I don't want to do anything that will hinder him from coming to know You."

As Phil was praying, he heard a knock on the door. There was Doug. "I hope you aren't mad at me," Doug said.

"Why would I be mad?"

"You made me that beautiful drawing, but things have been tight, and I didn't pay you for it. Here's the money I owe you, and a little more."

Etchings

A friend of Phil's, who was an engraver, asked Phil to do some sketches for him. While Phil was in his office, waiting for him, he noticed a dusty, old wooden cabinet. It contained old hand engraving tools that jewelers used to use before machines took over the engraving business. Phil had never seen such tools before. He picked one up and etched in a scrap of brass that was lying nearby. He made a little cartoon of Dave, the owner, who had stepped out of the office. When Dave returned, they had a laugh together over the cartoon. Then Phil said, "I really enjoy this. Can I take one of these?"

"Take them all," said Dave. "I don't know why I haven't thrown them out yet. Take some metal scraps too."

Phil took the tools and scraps home. He made a few wildlife sketches and brought them with him the next time he dropped in at Dave's shop.

Dave looked at them and said, "Do you have some time?"

"Sure," said Phil.

"I mean, can you go with me on a ride?"

"I guess. Where are we going?"

"Never mind. You'll see when we get there."

They went to a long-standing jewelry store in Omaha, one of Dave's usual stops for picking up engraving work. They went inside and visited with the jeweler. After a while, Dave pulled the engravings out of his pocket and showed them to the old man. "What do you think of that?" he asked.

"Nice," said the jeweler. "Who does that?"

"This guy," said Dave, pointing at Phil.

"How long have you been doing that?" the jeweler asked.

"A week," said Phil.

The jeweler laughed.

"No, really," Phil insisted.

"Well, maybe you should look into that," said the jeweler.

And so he did. "A man's gift maketh room for him, and bringeth him before great men" (Prov. 18:16).

Tammy asked Phil to etch a dog on one of the metal scraps. He did so, creating a detailed picture of a German Shepherd. She took the sample to a representative of the Nebraska Kennel Club and asked if she could set up a booth to sell engravings at their next dog show. Yes, she most certainly could.

When Phil came home that night, Tammy told him, "Honey, you have a few months to make some samples. We're going to the dog show in November." At the show, Tammy snapped photos of the show dogs and took orders for Phil to make engravings of the individual dogs for their owners.

Despite the added income, Tammy got a call from a bill collector. She had used a credit card to pay a utility bill, and she was getting deeper in the hole. When Phil came home from work, he found her distraught. "Honey, let's pray," he said. "God will take care of us."

They went to the bedroom and knelt to pray. They had just started when the phone rang in the kitchen. Phil got up to answer it. The man on the other end explained that he had seen Phil's engravings in an Omaha store. He was from One Box Pheasant Hunt, a hunting event that attracts wealthy sportsmen from all over the world. He wanted to hire Phil to make engravings as the prizes for the event.

"Before they call, I will answer; and while they are yet speaking, I will hear" (Isa. 65:24).

The representative came to the house to make arrangements with Phil. He saw Phil's bird dogs and asked, "Do you hunt?"

"Yeah."

"Do you want to be on a team?" As a side benefit for going on the hunt, Phil would have the opportunity to bring engravings to the banquet at the event. He agreed to go.

Phil and Tammy didn't have a car that they trusted to take them to Broken Bow, Nebraska, for the hunt. They borrowed a vehicle from their good friends, Ken and Carol Rempel. Other participants flew in private aircraft or came in fancy cars. They had high-end equipment and guns that cost more than Phil's house. Phil came wearing patched hunting pants and carrying an old gun. From a worldly perspective, Phil and Tammy were outclassed, but they were not out-hunted.

The first event was a trap shoot. Phil outshot everyone. The fancy dudes looked at each other. "Who is this bumble?"

Snow covered the ground the night before the hunt. The guide had arranged for the team to hunt in grassy fields, but the snow had packed the grass down. The pheasants weren't able to get into their usual lairs, so they stayed in the thickets. The team drove from field to field. By noon they still hadn't seen one pheasant. Phil didn't say anything, but he knew they weren't going to find anything in the snowy fields. Some of the other guys complained and cursed at the guide. When the truck arrived at another open field, the guys said they weren't getting out. Phil urged them not to quit, but they laughed at him. He got out of the truck and called to the other Nebraska guy on the team, "Ed, you coming with me?"

Ed saw what Phil saw. The tops of cedar trees in the distance. "Let's head towards that thicket," Phil said. "Every pheasant in the county is going to be in there."

Phil and Ed crossed the field and chased the pheasants out in droves. The other guys jumped out of the truck and ran across the field to join them. They shot enough pheasants to win first prize in the hunt.

At the awards banquet, Tammy sold every piece of artwork she and Phil had brought. One of the team members pulled Phil aside. He was a multimillionaire who led a loose life. He looked at Phil and said, "You don't drink?"

"No, I don't."

"Did you used to?"

"Yes, before I met Jesus, I did." Phil shared with him the joy and peace he found in Christ. This man later wrote and thanked Phil for the lessons that Phil taught him. He was especially impressed that when everyone else was grumbling, Phil didn't give up. He got out of the truck and kept plodding forward.

Phil attended the One Box Pheasant Hunt only one time, in 1990. Indeed, the rules of the event require each participant to come only once. Every year, however, from 1990-2022, Phil created brass etchings as the prizes for the event.

Jonathan Channing

After Tammy gave birth to her second child, she had three miscarriages. These happened relatively early in the pregnancy. With the first miscarriage, it was only after she passed a bloody mass that she realized that she had lost a child. Her sixth pregnancy continued normally into the second trimester. She went in for a routine doctor's visit, taking her two little ones with her. At the exam, no heartbeat could be found. The baby was dead.

Tammy went home, thinking she would pass the baby like she had the other miscarriages. Not so. She had a painful, eight-hour labor and delivered at the hospital. She and Phil went home without their child.

Phil and Tammy had agreed that the doctor could examine the baby. They wanted to know what was wrong. Why couldn't Tammy carry a child to term? But when they got home, they missed their baby, and they couldn't bear the thought of leaving him to be cut up and discarded in a dumpster. They needed to mourn over him and give him a proper burial. Phil called the hospital. "I'm coming to get my baby," he told the person who took the call.

"Umm, we can't do that," Phil was told.

"Life begins at conception," Phil said, "and I want to give my child a Christian burial."

The hospital staff told him, "We'll call you back." When the return call came, Phil was told that he couldn't just come and get the baby.

"What?" he retorted. "You can throw it in the incinerator. You can treat the child like trash, but as a parent, I can't come and get it?"

"We can only surrender the baby to a licensed mortician."

Phil called the undertaker who had buried Tammy's mom. He was a caring and reasonable man. He expressed his exasperation with the messed-up system and offered to get the baby for them.

"How much will it cost?" Phil asked.

"No charge."

The hospital told the mortician that for them to release the baby, he would have to provide them a plot number for the baby's burial. He called Phil and told him about this new hurdle. He had a plan. He would give the number for the plot Tammy's mom was buried in. They'd dig a shallow hole and put the baby in the same spot. The cemetery would charge $1,000 to dig the hole and bury the child. The mortician would charge nothing.

While Phil and Tammy were making plans to go ahead with this arrangement, Phil got another call. On the other end was the hushed voice of the head of pathology at the hospital.

"Are you Phil Kleymann? I heard about the confusion concerning the body of your child. How soon can you get to the hospital?"

"Thirty minutes."

She told him what door to use and said, "Meet me in the hall of the pathology department. I'll tell the guards to let you in."

Phil arrived at the hospital and told the guards he was Phil Kleymann. They snickered and let him in. He went to the appointed hallway. There was the head of pathology with a jar inside her lab coat. She gave it to Phil, saying, "Here's your child. Take your baby and go."

Tammy believed the baby was a boy. She and Phil named him Jonathan Channing. They took him up to a hill in the woods and found a tree where Phil had long before carved their names. They buried Jonathan under the tree, knowing they will see him again (2 Sam. 12:23).

Grandma's Passing

Grandma Louise was in her seventies when Phil and Tammy met her. She had lived a long life of service to the Lord, and she had grown in grace. Her younger days had been spent in a circle of churches known as *Gospel Halls*, and sometimes referred to as *tight* meetings. The gospel preached in this circle emphasized free grace through the work of Christ to the point that the necessity of repentance was generally omitted. Nonetheless, a high standard of living was expected of those who made a profession of knowing Christ. This incongruity produced a rigid atmosphere and an unperceived spirit of ritualistic legalism, even while preaching the true gospel of faith in Christ.

As she grew in grace, Louise had moved into the Open Brethren Assemblies with Bill and Mary Fear, who wanted to bring their daughters up in an atmosphere with more freedom. Grandma was unconscious of how much she had changed over the years and how the Spirit had softened her interactions with people and warmed her heart for the Scriptures. One day she discovered a recording of her late husband's preaching that had long been lost. When she listened to it, she was aghast at the somberness of the singing and the harshness of the preaching. She cut the tape into pieces and threw it away, telling her son, "I don't want young Christians like Tammy and Phil to hear it!"

Grandma died in 1998. She had requested a "short, simple ceremony where Christ alone is exalted." She asked Phil to preach, and specified that he include "a graphic description of the crucifixion."

"It is my desire," she wrote, "to have each one attending to fall in love with the man of Calvary." One of her sons suggested that she ask a family member to preach. She preferred Phil to do it, because he shared the warmth of heart-felt religion that she had imparted to him in her old age.

Work out your own salvation with fear and trembling.
—Philippians 2:12

CHAPTER 13

The Spirit at Work

Phil reminded Grandma of her husband, Harry, and it was her heart's desire that Phil continue the work that she and Harry had been involved in—following the Lord and teaching others to trust Him. She saw the Spirit at work in Phil's life and expressed the desire that a double portion of the Spirit would rest upon him and Tammy. That work included not just naming the name of Jesus, but observing all things that He commanded (Matt. 28:20). It included rejoicing in His first coming and looking for His second.

Phil and Tammy came to Christ in the early eighties, at a time when dispensationalist Bible teachers were predicting the soon return of Christ. The imminent rapture was often on their mind, and they talked about it frequently. When the Lord didn't come in 1988, the excitement wore off with many people, but with each passing year, the imminency of the Lord's coming only accelerates. The stage is being set for the events prophesied in the Bible. The urgency to preach the gospel and see loved ones safely walking in the truth increases more and more. By keeping their eyes on eternity, Phil and Tammy have maintained a fervent testimony for Christ, and an expectancy for His return.

The Bible Chapel which the Kleymanns attended did not have a paid pastor. The men of the church took turns preaching. Phil's gift as a public speaker had been evident at his wedding, and he started preaching very early in his Christian experience. As he grew in understanding, he took on the work of an elder.

Phil worked as a truck driver, hauling loads in the Midwest. The Lord enabled him to share the good news of Jesus Christ with many on the road, and he had the joy of leading some drivers to Christ.

Smiley

Smiley was a driver from Kansas City. He hit Des Moines, Iowa, at the same time as Phil. They talked on the radio as they made their way to Minneapolis. After dropping their loads, they had breakfast together before heading home again. During these times together, Phil talked about the Lord Jesus and His power to save.

One day, on the way to their terminal, Smiley saw a vehicle in a car lot that interested him. He asked Phil to drive over there with him, to look at the car. The car lot was closed, but the door to the car was unlocked, so Smiley opened it and looked inside. In the car was a pamphlet by William MacDonald, a Bible teacher with whom Phil was acquainted.

"Hey, look at this," Smiley said. "It's something about the Bible! Do you think this guy will mind if I take it?"

"I don't think he will mind," said Phil with a grin.

Smiley took the pamphlet, and through reading it, came to faith in Christ. No doubt the owner of the car lot rejoiced when the two men returned to tell him what had happened.

Racecar Driver

When delivering to a concrete company in Blair, Nebraska, Phil visited with an older guy named Bob who had raced stock cars in his younger years. Phil asked him if he had heard of Sunset Speedway outside of Omaha.

"Sunset? Yeah, I raced the first race they ever had in 1967."

"Did you know Don Culbertson?" asked Phil.

"Did you know Don?" Bob asked.

"Yeah, Don was my neighbor."

"Come to my office," said Bob.

Phil went to the office where Bob showed him a photo of an upside-down race car in flames. There was someone in the car and another man kneeling beside it. In the background were some guys standing by a pick-up, watching from a safe distance.

"That's me in the car," Bob explained. He choked up as he went on, "That man kneeling beside me is Don Culbertson. Don was my friend. He's cutting me free with a knife. He risked his life to save me. His hands were burned getting me out, and he had scars for the rest of his life. See the guys in the back? They are the track stewards, hired by the racetrack to come to the aid of a driver in trouble. They weren't there. They weren't going to risk it. That car was going to blow up any minute. Don was there because he was my friend."

"Bob, do you read the Bible?" Phil asked. "Read John 10; your story is there:"

> I am the good shepherd: the good shepherd giveth his life for the sheep. But he that is an hireling, and not the shepherd, whose own the sheep are not, seeth the wolf coming, and leaveth the sheep, and fleeth: and the wolf catcheth them, and scattereth the sheep. The hireling fleeth, because he is an hireling, and careth not for the sheep. I am the good shepherd, and know my sheep, and am known of mine. As the Father knoweth me, even so know I the Father: and I lay down my life for the sheep (John 10:11-15).

Aztec Mike

Phil's truck routes were semi-local. He was on the road a couple days at a time. He had Sundays free for church, and he had regular intervals at home with his family every week. He was at home when a telemarketer called and Tammy jumped at the chance to have her carpets cleaned. A man came over and shampooed the rugs. When he was done, he got out his paperwork and wanted Phil and Tammy to sign on the dotted line for a six-hundred-dollar vacuum cleaner. They really could not afford it. They told him, "We never make a decision without praying. Give us a day or two."

"Are you Christians?" he asked. "Where do you fellowship?" He was new to the area and looking for a church.

Phil told him the name, time, and location of their church.

On Sunday morning, there was a stir in the back of the chapel. In came Mike Herron in bib overalls, covered in tattoos, with cigarettes in his shirt sleeve. "The Kirby vacuum cleaner guy is here!" Tammy told Phil in an excited whisper.

Mike had been wearing a suit and tie in his role as a salesman. He intentionally chose less polished apparel to test the church's reaction. Apparently, it passed his test. He loved the chapel.

Mike had been born in the Bronx, New York. He ran away from a foster home when seven years old. After living on the streets, he got involved with the Hell's Angels who dubbed him, "Aztec Mike."

While riding with the gang, Mike got involved in a fight and killed a man. He was caught and convicted of second-degree murder. While in prison for this offense, someone threw a Bible through the prison bars. With nothing else to do, Mike started reading it. He came to the crucifixion of Christ and was furious about the injustice that was done to the Lord. When he realized that Christ had been killed for him, his heart was changed. He didn't know what had happened, but he knew that something had happened to him. The prisoners around him knew it too.

When Mike got out of prison, he wanted to find Christians, so he looked for a church. He figured he'd find the most

Christians at the biggest church. When he went in, however, the people scattered. He was devastated. Having no family but the Hells Angels, he turned to them.

Mike's brothers in the gang had kept his bike for him. They took him in, and he rode with them. Without Christian fellowship, his growth was slow, but his love for Christ was vibrant. He talked about his newfound faith, and some of his fellow bikers embraced the Savior. He became known as a preacher, and on the rare occasion when someone in the group wanted to be married, Mike performed the wedding.

When Mike came to Omaha, he was struggling with alcohol, and he wanted freedom. Mary Fear had been working on a Christian recovery program, combining Biblical truth with some of the elements of a twelve-step program, but she herself had no experience with the issue. In Phil's words, "She had never been any closer to a beer bottle than to the NASA space shuttle, but she knew the Scriptures." Mary hadn't yet used her program with anyone. Mike became her first student. The Scriptures enabled him to get the victory he longed for. He helped Mary adjust her terminology and perfect her program, called Overcomers in Christ.[3] Mike promoted this organization, and became the spokesman for it.

Mike went into the jails and prisons around Omaha, preaching Christ. He later moved to Missouri and continued his work, promoting the recovery program and preaching in jails. When he died, over six hundred people attended his funeral. Many of them were men he had led to Christ.

Youth Group

The Kleymanns opened their home for the work of the Lord. Tammy has a gift for hospitality, and she used it to further her opportunities for evangelism. They had people in frequently, as they had learned from Grandma. They also had youth group meetings in their basement.

While their kids were growing up, Phil and Tammy had foreign exchange students stay with them over the school year. Some of these responded to the preaching of God's Word. Those who didn't still appreciated the hospitality provided, with one notable exception. A young man from Germany expected to be waited upon. When he didn't get his way, he marched down to the coordinator's house and demanded that he be moved to another house. The coordinator told him, "If you can't get along with those people, you can't get along with anyone. If you don't want to stay, I can send you home." He stayed, but the living arrangement was a challenge for everyone.

Exchange students were invited to church, but they were not required to attend. They were expected to attend youth group, however. Phil taught from the Scriptures at these meetings. The kids talked about the relevancy of Scripture and about its relation to current events. Besides the kids in their chapel, young people from other churches who were serious about learning the Bible came to the Kleymann's youth group meetings.

One teenage girl from the Kleymann's church family, who was influenced by goth culture, came regularly to the youth group. She shared what she was learning with a friend she had met downtown. Her philosophically-minded friend had neo-Nazi leanings. He poo-poohed what she told him, so she invited him to come to the youth group and set Phil straight. He agreed.

When the pair arrived a little late, they looked so unlike youth-group kids that Tammy's sister, Kim, who was visiting, wasn't sure if she should let them in. The girl was dressed all in black, and her friend sported numerous piercings. Tammy welcomed them in and brought them downstairs.

The young man's neo-Nazi philosophy melted away under the overwhelming power of the Word of God. He kept coming back to the youth group, and in a few weeks, he became a

Christian. The girl dressed in goth attire was also solidly converted to Christ. The two of them married, and they seek to honor the Lord with their lives.

Before Phil and Tammy took over the youth group, the weekly meetings were held at Ken and Carol Rempel's house. Ken was in charge, but Phil did some of the preaching. One pleasant evening, Phil gave a Bible lesson on Ken's back porch. The neighbor lady, Sharon, was outside doing yard work. Sharon had heard the gospel from her sister, but she was resisting it. She heard Phil talking about the reasons that people reject God's Word. Her spirit was stirred, and she pulled up a chair to listen from the other side of a privacy fence. The next day, she went to the Rempels and sheepishly told them, "I don't want to be a snoopy neighbor, but last night I listened to what was being said. Can I come to the youth group?"

As an adult, Sharon attended the youth group, listening to Phil's teachings. She also started going to Sunday church. She became a solid and devoted Christian until she went home to be with the Lord.

Demons

A young man, whom Tammy had led to Christ, and who fellowshipped at the chapel, asked the church members to pray for his mother. She came from a background where there was demonic activity, and she had been acting strangely. She had been found tearing down the neighbor's rock wall. Another time she was digging in the sod at the neighbor's house. Unbeknownst to anyone, her daughter had had an abortion. Emotionally distressed over having killed her baby, she gave the baby a name. No one knew its name or even knew of its existence, but her mother was found hammering out the floor drain in the basement, because she heard a baby crying for her. Its name was the secret name of her unknown grandchild.

The Spirit at Work

One hot Saturday night Phil got a call. The man and his wife were bringing his mother out to see them. She had been in the attic, clothed in shorts and a tank top, swimming in fiberglass insulation, looking for the baby.

The afflicted woman, her son and daughter-in-law, and Phil and Tammy sat down in the sunroom at the back of the house, overlooking the fields. No neighbors could be seen. Phil asked the woman if she had ever trusted in Christ as her savior.

She hadn't.

Phil asked, "Can we read from the Bible?"

He opened the Bible and invited the woman to read. She started to do so, but very soon her natural voice was taken over by a deep, mocking, and vulgar voice. When this voice got to the name of God or Jesus in a Bible verse, it would begin to choke and dry heave. It would not finish the verse.

Phil and Tammy remained calm. They felt sad, but not afraid. Phil told the spirit, "Jesus is Lord of this home." Naming the woman, he told the demon that she was welcome. "You are not."

"Down the drain!" was the response.

Phil said, "We will wait." This happened over and over again.

Occasionally the woman would burst into tears and cry, "That's not me. I'm so sorry."

"Do you want to trust Christ?" Phil asked.

"Yes."

But then the spirit would be back.

"What's your name?" Phil asked.

The woman leaned toward him and got in his face, hers contorted. "You think I'm alone?" the voice sneered. "There are hundreds of us! I'll tell the rest to go, but I'm staying. She promised to marry me."

This went on all night, back and forth like an arm-wrestling match. There seemed to be a stalemate. Everyone was worn out. About 5:00 a.m., Tammy called a man from the church and told him to wake everyone in the church and ask them to pray. The Christians responded, and a heavenly host showed up in response to their prayers.

The distraught woman was sitting on her haunches, looking out the glass doors at the darkness all around and screaming in the vulgar voice, "They're all around us!"

At first, Tammy thought the woman was seeing demons. She shut the blinds and went through the house, praying in the name of Jesus. Then she turned on some hymn music and sat back down.

Suddenly, the woman collapsed on the couch and shouted in her own voice, "Get the Bible. They're gone!" It was angels, not demons, who had surrounded them. The angels had angered and frightened the demons who had been tormenting her. After crying out in rage, they had finally left.

After going through some Scriptures, the relieved woman exclaimed, "He died for me!" She went home happy. She apologized to her husband for her unfaithfulness, and her demons never came back. She expressed a desire for others to know Christ, and she never let go of her profession of faith. Nonetheless, she did not lead the life of victory that was available to her in Christ, and she died an early death.

For whatsoever is born of God overcometh the world: and this is the victory that overcometh the world, even our faith.
—1 John 5:4

CHAPTER 14

Chalk Talks and Camp Work

The church that Phil and Tammy attended expected the men of the congregation to take part in the preaching. Most of the men in the assembly were young and didn't have much speaking experience, so Bill Fear arranged for Leonard Lindsted to come for a weeklong homiletics course. When Leonard found out that Phil was an artist, he asked Phil if he was interested in learning to do chalk talks.

"Sure," said Phil.

"I'll drop something off for you," said Leonard.

A week or so later, in 1985, some guys showed up at Phil's door and surprised him with an old chalkboard and a booklet by Leonard Lindsted called, "The Chalk that Talks." Besides these, there was a personal letter filled with Leonard's dry humor that struck a chord with Phil. Leonard wrote, "I hope I don't smother you, but better you than s'mother guy." He had drawn a cartoon of a big rug with a lump in the middle and hands sticking out from under it. The blurb said, "I, Leonard Lindsted, do mantle thee."

Someone from Willowbrook Bible Camp in Des Moines, Iowa, heard that Phil was starting to do chalk talks. They asked him to come to camp. He and Tammy hardly knew what they were getting into, but they felt the call of God and didn't dare decline.

Camp was challenging, but equally rewarding. Tammy was as much involved as Phil. She had a knack for finding the kids who had been abused. Hurting girls, who didn't dare speak up in most circumstances, bared their souls to her. Phil's engaging presentations kept the kids' attention as he labored the basic points of the gospel. The campers, awakened to their need of Christ, gathered around to hear more. Phil and Tammy opened the Word of God on a personal level and showed individual kids the provision that Christ had made for them.

Jeanetta Vanderhart from Pella, Iowa, paid the way for troubled kids to go to Willowbrook to hear the gospel. It was a rough and needy crowd at the camp. The Spirit attended Phil's labors, and some of the kids yielded to the truth they heard. One, who had been in a coven and was cutting herself, was liberated by the truth of Jesus Christ. Many others also made professions of salvation.

Phil and Tammy had found their calling. Phil did more and more chalk talks at summer camps, weekend outreaches, vacation Bible school, and whatever other opportunity he was given. Both he and Tammy did personal work wherever they went.

Chip

At one of the first camps the Kleymanns went to, there was a troubled boy from a Christian family. Chip couldn't look an adult in the eye, and he stayed away from the preacher. He always sat in the very back of the chapel. He had "Poison" written on his shoes. He confided in his counselor that he was having terrible dreams about killing the camp director with a knife.

Chalk Talks and Camp Work

On Thursday night, the speakers and camp staff were having a time of prayer together after the kids had gone to bed. While they were praying, they heard someone run into the chapel. Chip burst into the room in a fit of hysteria. He fell on his counselor's lap crying, "It happened again!"

He was holding a paper on which he had scribbled, "How old do you have to be to believe in God? The Ouija board never lies. Die, die, die. Help me!"

Phil asked Chip what he had written on the paper. Chip didn't know. Phil asked, "What's your name?"

"Chip."

"Are there times you get angry and you don't know why?"

Chip set his jaw, got close to Phil's face, and rubbing his temples, he said, "Sometimes I get **so-o-o-o-o** angry."

"Do you know why you wrote, "Help me?"

"No."

"Have you ever asked God for help?"

"I don't know."

"Have you ever trusted Jesus as your Savior?"

"I don't know."

Phil told him that the Lord Jesus had died to save him, and that He would help anyone who came to Him. He gave him some Scriptures to read. Then he told him, "I want you to go to the kitchen and tell God you want His help."

The next morning at chapel, Chip sat in the front row. Afterward, he approached Phil and told him that he had trusted Jesus as his Savior.

Chip's bunkmate approached Phil, too. The little guy was troubled about Chip. He said, "Chip told me bad stories. I was scared. He curled up in a ball and started moaning. I touched him, and he sat up. He jumped all the way over the bunk. He grabbed a paper and pen and wrote something. I asked him if he was OK. He jumped again and hit his head on the ceiling. Then he looked at the paper and started crying. Then, he ran out of the cabin. What do you think happened?"

"I don't know," said Phil, "But do you know where he went? He ran right to us. We were praying. We told him about Jesus. He had never trusted Christ to be his Savior. But he says he did last night."

The wide-eyed little boy said, "He did? I'm so glad, Mr. Phil!"

"Maybe Chip will be different now. You watch and see."

At the campfire that night, Chip gave his testimony of finding peace in Christ.

Golden Image

One of the chalk talks that Phil developed was on the golden image in the book of Daniel. This was intended as a discipleship message for teenagers. He described how the crowd bowed down to the image Nebuchadnezzar had made when the music played, ignorant of the wickedness that it stood for. He compared this to what goes on at a rock concert. "What's the message at rock concerts?" he asked. "Death, perversion, and anti-God. You don't want to be in that crowd. But when you say no to them, it is going to cost you, like it did Daniel's three friends (Dan. 3). They said no to the crowd and had to go through the fire, but the Lord showed up, as He always does for those who trust in Him."

The son of a Presbyterian preacher had come to camp with rock music in his suitcase. At campfire after this message was preached, he brought his KISS albums and with tears streaming from his eyes, he threw them in the fire. He testified to having trusted Christ. His dad called Phil later and said, "You don't know me, but you know my son. What did you tell him? He is a new kid. He came home from camp and tore down his rock posters. I want to thank you!"

Mila

Mila came to a week-long camp with a sister who had driven the two of them there with a friend. The older sister did not appreciate camp. "Sin and death, sin and death, that's all they talk about here," she said. On Wednesday she decided to leave.

Thursday morning Phil sat outside the chapel building. He saw Mila coming around the corner, dragging her suitcase. "Mila, are you leaving?" he asked.

"Yeah, we're leaving. We don't want to stay," she replied.

"Oh, I'm so sorry to hear that. Before you leave, can I spend one or two minutes with you to tell you something that's so important?"

Mila paused and looked toward the parking lot where her sister was waiting. "Well, OK," she said.

"I want to tell you something from God's word that you can take home with you. The Bible says you and me are the same."

"It does?"

"Yeah, we all have something. It's a big, big problem. You've got it, and I've got it. You know what I've got and I know what you've got. It's called sin. It's the thing that makes our conscience go off. We know it's there. But it's bigger than we know, because that sin, God doesn't have it. Because of that, we're separated from Him. He loves us but it comes between Him and us. What He wants you to know as you leave, is that He loves you so much. Let me show you how much He loves you."

Phil turned to John 3:16. "I want you to read this," he told her. "But I don't want you to read it without putting your name in there. Who is God talking to? It says 'the world,' but right now He is talking to Mila. Put your name in there."

Mila read, "For God so loved Mila that He gave His only begotten Son that if Mila believes on Him, Mila will not perish but have everlasting life."

Phil watched as the look on her face brightened. She looked up at him with tears in her eyes.

"God loves you, Mila. Jesus died for you. Take that home with you. Heaven is wide open for you."

Mila thanked him, looking at him with questioning eyes as if to say, "Now what do I do?"

The older sister was gunning the car's engine. Mila walked out to the parking lot. The car drove away, but Mila came back. Phil said to her, "I thought you were leaving."

"I'm not leaving. I'm staying."

"I'm glad to hear that."

"My sister said, 'Get in the car, Mila. They're cramming this stuff down your throat.' I told her, 'No, they're not. I'm eating it up, and I'm loving it.'"

On Friday night around the campfire, Mila gave her testimony. She said, "You know what it felt like when I got saved? It felt like the day my dad took me deer hunting. A snow storm hit, and we got lost in the woods. The wind was blowing, and we couldn't see. My dad tried not to act scared, but I know he was. We were walking in circles, and I knew we were in trouble. Our cell phone wouldn't work. Finally we came out into a clearing, and there on the top of a hill we saw a light. I never forgot how happy I was to see that light. It was my mom's car! That's exactly what it felt like the other day when I saw God's light."

Ryan

Many of the campers do not open their hearts to the gospel. Ryan is one of the saddest examples. After a chalk talk, as the chairs were being rearranged for a game, Tammy's Bible was placed on the floor. Ryan went over to it and stomped on it. Tammy said, "That's my Bible!"

He didn't care.

"That's God's word," said Tammy, "He loves you."
"I don't care."
She had to let it go.

A few years later, the boy drowned in a farm pond in Iowa. His artwork was displayed at his funeral. One of his drawings was of a pond with an island. About half way to the island, there was a hand sticking out of the water. The caption on the drawing had been written in the form of a newspaper heading. It gave his last name and then, "Dies in '95."

Ryan had prophesied his own death. In the summer of 1995, he was swimming to an island with some friends. About half way there, he cried out, struggling. One of the other boys swam over to him, but he was unable to save him. He said it felt as though something were pulling Ryan down. When his body was found, there were mysterious puncture wounds in his feet, and his fingertips were black.

Justin

Rick, a rough oil-field worker whom Phil had known as a boy, moved into the neighborhood of the church that Phil and Tammy attended. He brought his wife and family to check out the place. When they left, they said to one another, "Those people have something we need."

Phil invited the older son, Justin, to camp.

At camp, Justin learned that Jesus, who had come to die, was coming back again. Fear of the second coming of Christ hit him so hard that he became physically ill. One morning after a chalk talk, he excused himself from the games and went to his cabin, his mind filled with questions. He fell asleep and had a terrifying dream in which the Lord came to rapture the church, and he wasn't ready. Within a day or two he put his faith in Christ.

Justin went home from camp with both barrels loaded with the gospel. He told his mom and dad plainly that they had better get ready for the Lord's return. They were pleased with the changes they saw in their son, and they started attending church regularly. Within a few weeks, Rick embraced the gospel of Christ.

A little later, Phil preached about Mary Magdalene, a wicked woman who was converted and became a blessing to Christ. She was one of the last people at the cross and the first at His tomb. The message was accompanied with extraordinary power from the Holy Spirit. When Phil was done speaking, the congregation stayed silently glued to their seats. Finally, one of the men said, "Let's sing," and called out *Blessed Assurance*. In the middle of this song, Rick's wife broke down in tears and wept on his shoulder. She also put her faith in Christ.

The pistol-packing grandma in this family occasionally came up from Oklahoma to visit. She attended the church services with them. She watched as the men stood up one by one and testified to the love of God as demonstrated by the cross. She realized that though she was evangelical in her beliefs, she had never understood the beauty of the cross the way these men did. In her own words, "I realized for me the blood wasn't red. It was black and white to me." She came under the conviction that there was something missing in her faith. With joy, she later came to church with the news, "The blood is red for me!'

Justin, however, did not maintain his joy in the Lord. When he moved out of his parents' home, he wandered down a path dishonoring to the Lord and adopted a sinful lifestyle. While still a young man in his twenties, he contracted an aggressive lung cancer. Six weeks from his diagnosis, he died.

The night before Justin died, he called for Phil. He didn't ask for healing. He knew he was dying, and he knew why. He confessed that he had been living wrong and that God was righteous to chasten him. He said, "God loves me. Whom He loves, He chastens."

But watch thou in all things, endure afflictions, do the work of an evangelist, make full proof of thy ministry. —2 Timothy 4:5

CHAPTER 15

Page Turners

The day after Phil was saved, his heart for fishing kicked in. He took his Bible and a six pack of beer to witness to the guys at work. One of the guys was awakened to his need of Christ, and Phil's lifelong career as an evangelist and Bible teacher began.

Phil and Tammy followed Grandma's example of hospitality to promote the Lord's work. They had people into their home and opened the Bible with them. Over the years, they have led many people to Christ, using the written Word. Each of them has their favorite verses to use, and they each have their own system based on what they learned from Grandma. They modify it, of course, according to the needs of their listeners.

There is no magic formula for bringing a soul to Christ. Having a system for going through the Scriptures with a seeking soul is a starting point and an aid to gospel work. It can never become a formality or a ritual. Every soul is different, and each one must have his own dealings directly with God. Phil and Tammy's goal is to facilitate this process, much like a midwife aiding a physical birth.

One of Tammy's greatest fears is giving someone a false sense of security. She is very careful not to pronounce anyone saved. She never tells a person they are or are not saved. She leads them to the Scripture and allows them to draw their own conclusion.

One of the most challenging aspects of gospel work is standing back and allowing God to work in a person's heart as only He knows how to do. He alone can read the secret thoughts of the heart. When a child is convulsed in tears over the thought of eternal damnation, the temptation to provide comfort can be nearly overwhelming, but there is great danger in providing that comfort prematurely. Phil and Tammy are especially careful not to force a stillbirth in which a person goes through the motions of being born again but has no true life. They are painfully aware that it can and does happen, but they do their best not to be the cause of it.

Scripture

Confidence in the Bible as the Word of God is an essential starting point for working with a soul. Tammy asks an inquirer, "Can you believe everything in this Book?"

If the person hesitates, Tammy takes them through the prophetic verses concerning Christ's first coming, such as Micah 5:2. Only when she has established the reliability of the Scriptures, does she move forward with its message to the sinner.

"What's so special about this Book?" She asks, then proceeds in simple, child-like words to tell how it changed her life. "It's God's love letter to you," she says. "He came to earth as a man, but He went back to heaven. He is not coming back until He comes in judgment. He can't have a face-to-face conversation with you, but He left you a letter. In this letter there is something very important that He wants you to know. Do you know what it is?"

Tammy then turns to 1 John 5:9-13. Gently, she stops on each verse, making sure her listener understands. Without pressure, but with emotional intensity, she makes the message personal to them.

> If we receive the witness of men, the witness of God is greater: for this is the witness of God which he hath testified of his Son (v. 9).

She has the person read this verse and asks them what a witness of men is. To help young people understand, she will give the example of a newspaper or website giving the scores to the high school game they missed. Can this testimony be trusted? So much more the word of God.

> He that believeth on the Son of God hath the witness in himself: he that believeth not God hath made him a liar; because he believeth not the record that God gave of his Son. And this is the record, that God hath given to us eternal life, and this life is in his Son (vv. 10-11).

"Do you believe what God says about His Son? 'He that hath the Son hath life; and he that hath not the Son of God hath not life'" (v. 12).

"Everyone is included in this verse. Either you have the Son and have life or you do not have the Son and you do not have life. Do you have life?"

> These things have I written unto you that believe on the name of the Son of God; that ye may know that ye have eternal life, and that ye may believe on the name of the Son of God (v. 13).

After having the person read this verse aloud, putting their own name in place of the applicable pronouns, Tammy turns the person to Ephesians 2:8-9:

> For by grace are ye saved through faith; and that not of yourselves: it is the gift of God: Not of works, lest any man should boast.

"How are you saved?" she asks and makes the listener stick to the text. It is the gift of God, by grace, through faith, not of works. Then she moves to 1 Peter 2:24:

> Who his own self bare our sins in his own body on the tree, that we, being dead to sins, should live unto righteousness: by whose stripes ye were healed.

This verse may need some explaining for people to understand. She clarifies that it is talking about Christ and explains that *bare* means to *carry*. At this point, Tammy presents a drawing of the backside of the crucifixion. She pulls out a blank sheet of paper and draws a timeline on it. She puts the person's name at the top and their birthdate at the beginning of the line. She asks for the date of their death. Of course, they don't know that. She talks about how uncertain life is. Death could come at any time.

Most of the young people who come to Tammy feel the weight of their sins. In some cases, Tammy may have to turn to the lists of sins in the New Testament. To experience a solid conversion from darkness to light, a person must realize that he is a sinner and begin to understand how sinful sin really is.

Tammy asks inquirers if they sin. She proposes that perhaps they have sinned twice a day and multiplies that times the years of their life. If a person sins only two times a day, in ten years, that's 7,300 sins. Those of us who know ourselves realize that we are guilty of many more than this. Tammy writes the number on the paper and asks if a person can get to heaven with those sins. She folds up the paper and places it on the picture of Christ on the cross.

"Where are your sins?" she asks.

When people seem to have embraced the truth of the gospel, she takes them to Psalm 103:12, "As far as the east is from the west, so far hath he removed our transgressions from us."

Tammy gives the person more verses to mediate on. Some kids are very emotional. Others are stoic. The state of their emotions has little bearing on where they are with Christ. Tammy rejoices to be able to take people through the Scriptures, but she doesn't count conversions. Often it isn't until much later that she finds out a child she dealt with at camp has come to Christ. Other times she sees the light come on in their minds and believes it has been embraced in their hearts.

No matter how old a person is, they cannot meet with the Living God and not have their life changed. Some show more fruit than others, but turning toward the Savior of sinners requires a person to turn away from themselves and their sin. This happens in the heart. Sometimes the fruit of it is seen right away. Other times the seed seems to lie dormant in the earth for a season before springing up in the fullness of life.

Follow me, and I will make you fishers of men.
—Matthew 4:19

CHAPTER 16

Testimonies

The results of any efforts to preach the gospel are in God's hands. He works by the power of His Holy Spirit through vessels, such as Phil and Tammy, who yield themselves to Him. The primary gratitude of those who have been saved from their sins belongs to God, the great giver who gave His only Son for the redemption of all who will trust Him.

The overflow of thankful hearts goes to those, who under God, have been used to awaken and turn us from our misery to hope in Christ Jesus, the Lord. Many people have cause to thank God for calling Phil and Tammy to be fishers of men and entrusting them with the message of redemption. Many who have been given hope and had their lives changed by the gospel preached by Phil and Tammy express their thankfulness for the messengers as well as the message. A sampling of these have provided personal testimonies to the goodness of God towards them.

Recently when the Phil and Tammy were at a camp in Missouri, a mother brought her children to see Phil and Tammy. They barely remembered her, but she had been saved by listening to the chalk talks when she was a pre-teen. When she went home from camp, her dad noticed a change in her. Through her, he was also drawn to the Savior. This testimony is from her:

Renee Groene

 I grew up just miles away from Turkey Hill Ranch Bible Camp. When I was ten years old, in the summer of 1992, I could not be more excited that my parents were allowing me to attend.

 I took my cousin Stacey with me, and we were about to embark on something much bigger than a fun week of summer camp. Turkey Hill was wonderful, everything from the staff, the counselors, the speaker, and the campers. I did not personally know any of the staff, but I was fortunate enough to meet Phil and Tammy. Phil was the head speaker that week and I was lucky enough to get his wife, Tammy, as my counselor! My bunkmates and I thought we were extra special because we had the speaker's wife as our cabin counselor. We took in all the activities that camp had to offer, and boy did we have fun. All the while we were learning of the Lord and His love, mercy, and grace for us. Tammy and Phil took us exploring at the creek and on a cave hike. They showed us love and understanding. They were so compassionate and relatable.

 As each day passed, I could feel something changing in my spirit. I was a little fearful with all this new knowledge I was learning. Each day, Phil gave a chalk talk that would reveal Jesus Christ and the urgency of the time. He was so creative with his drawings; I can still vividly remember so many of the lessons he shared. My all-time favorite was the thieves on the cross with Jesus as He was crucified. Each day we would have daily devotions after chapel. He would dissect and answer any questions we may have or want to share. Most of the time I sat quietly listening and all the while knowing the Lord was tugging on my spirit. Near the end of week, I gave my life to the Lord. It was after chapel one evening with Phil and Tammy. They led me to the Lord right there. Just as I was, no bells, no whistles. Just as I am.

Camp soon wrapped up, and I could not wait to share my newfound love of the Lord with my family. Before I left camp, I asked if I could take home one of the camp's extra Bibles and give it to my dad, as I was unsure if he had one. Weeks after camp had wrapped up, I was still singing the songs I had learned, doing the motions, and sharing Phil's chalk talks.

My Father had grown up in the Methodist church and attended regularly. I would attend the early morning Catholic church service with my mom and then come home and attend a service later that same morning with my dad. I loved it. My Dad and I would talk about the sermons, and soon we would both be drawn closer to the Lord. Although my dad had attended church his whole life, he truly accepted Christ that same summer that I returned home from camp. Fast forward some 20 years later, and my dad is now the Pastor of the Assembly of God church I attend.

I am so thankful for my many summers spent at camp. Each year I would make sure I chose the week of camp that Phil was speaking. I am now forty-two, and my daughter has had the privilege to meet Phil and Tammy and sit under their teachings at camp. They truly changed my life, and they were largely responsible for my accepting Christ. God is Good.

During the same period, another young girl, who did not have encouragement from her parents, found hope and purpose in the truth of the gospel.

Erin Strawn

The year was 1992. I was twelve. It started off as a painful summer for me. This was the first time I was not allowed to go to the camp I had always gone to. I also wasn't allowed to go to my last year of swimming lessons to be certified before a lifeguard. But for some odd reason, when I asked to go to this camp that Tammy and Phil were doing, I was allowed to go. Both my sister and I went. Total God thing!

One night at camp, before we headed to our cabins, we were asked, "If you died tonight, do you know where you will go?"

I said, "I guess, Heaven." But it is not enough to just guess! So, I prayed all night.

The next day Tammy took me aside for a walk through the *Romans Road*. Without knowing why, she took me to a passage she didn't normally use, John 14:1-6. I was struck by verse six where Jesus says, "I am the way, the truth, and the life: no man cometh unto the Father, but by me."

When I heard this, I bawled and bawled.

I accepted Jesus as my personal Savior.

When I got back from camp and as soon as I got in the car I said, "Mom! I got saved!"

She said, "I knew I shouldn't have sent you."

The story doesn't end there. Even though I wasn't allowed to go to any more camps, church groups, etc., I knew Jesus. I have grown so much in Him. If it wasn't for Tammy's faithfulness that day, would I be where I am today? Would I know the Truth? I am so thankful for Phil and Tammy and will never forget how their selflessness brought me the best gift of my entire life!

Daniel Ginn

I grew up in a home where my parents loved each other and loved the Lord. My mom was raised Lutheran and my dad put his faith in Jesus in order to marry my mom. At some point, their simple faith grew into something good. They were first generation Christians when it came to genuine faith, not just religion.

Josh

My parents did their best to teach me about the Bible and who Jesus is. We attended a large charismatic church in Omaha that was good about worshiping God. It was a loving church, but I wasn't plugged in enough to realize I was missing something.

At church we spent forty-five minutes or more singing worship songs. The pastor would then speak. He shared a captivating story or an illustration. Sometimes he had a movie clip that fit his topic. He read a verse and talked, but he never really dug into Scripture in a way that went home to my heart.

I heard that I needed to ask Jesus into my heart to be saved from hell, so I would lay in bed many nights with my arms wide open. I was waiting for something magical to happen or some feeling to occur. Nothing happened, and I doubted.

Perhaps I was saved at a younger age, but it didn't click until years later. My best friend since kindergarten was Josh Kleymann. I got to know his parents, Phil and Tammy, well over the years. Josh invited me to Willowbrook Bible Camp, and I went there almost every year from middle school on.

The summer after my eighth grade, Phil was preaching at camp. He asked the question, "Do you know for sure where you are going to spend eternity?"

I thought to myself, "I think so."

Phil said, "It shouldn't be, 'I think so.'"

I thought, "Ummm, I hope so."

Phil, as if he were reading my mind, said, "It shouldn't be 'I hope so.' It should be, 'I know so!'"

I realized that I did not know for certain. So I stayed afterwards and talked with Phil and Tammy that night. I believe Tammy shared with me some verses like Romans 3:23, 6:23, 5:8, Ephesians 2:8-9, and others. I knew I was a sinner. I knew my sins meant death in hell. I knew God loved me and sent Jesus to die for me, and I knew salvation was by faith alone in Him. But I needed to hear 1 John 5:13, which says,

> I write these things to you who believe in the name of the Son of God, that you may know that you have eternal life (NKJV).

When they gave me that verse, I walked away, not just knowing the knowledge of who Jesus was, but truly believing it to be true to me. Not my parents' faith, not my friends' faith, not anyone else's faith, but my own. I was different. A seed of faith and a new confidence that could never be taken away had been planted in me.

I was involved in different youth groups and Bible studies throughout junior high and high school. My sophomore year, my youth group decided to go on a short-term mission trip to Trinidad and Tobago. While I was there, the Lord used me to help lead someone to Jesus. Me? An ineloquent high-schooler with a fumbling tongue? Yes, even me!

The team went to the same place a year later and witnessed this man's baptism. He had led others to the Lord—all because I was willing to be used. God did the work. I wanted more of that.

After high school, I went to Emmaus Bible College for four years. I met my wife there. I graduated with a youth ministry degree and moved back to Omaha. In 2009, God called us to be the directors at the very camp where I had gotten saved, Willowbrook Bible Camp.

From there he called us to youth ministry in Glenwood, Iowa. God is good. He is still teaching us many hard things. I wouldn't change it for the world.

Shane Snipes

Growing up, I was raised by a very strict stepfather. He taught me a lot about the Bible and God, but the only thing I could ever remember was being afraid of God. I knew he was going to judge me for the way I was living my life. It wasn't until I was 11 that I was taught about the love of God, and how much God wanted a relationship with me. My dear friend Phil opened his Bible after one of his chalk talks and showed me John 3:16. He covered the word *whosoever* and replaced it with my name. He read it over and over. It absolutely blew my mind! I was totally missing the big picture! God loves me, and wants to be with me!

As time went on, our family got in the habit of NOT attending church. Eventually we totally separated ourselves from the whole thing. That started a complete downward spiral for our family. My parents got divorced, and my brother and I started living for the world. I ended up having two kids before I was twenty! The whole time I knew what I was doing was wrong, but I continued to reject God and his plans for me.

One Saturday morning, my stepbrother, stepfather, and I were out hunting in the middle of nowhere, somewhere in Iowa. We came across a field with two men hunting a creek line. All we could see was their vehicle and two small specks walking in the field. As these two men started walking toward us. I couldn't help but stare at their vehicle. It was a maroon Toyota SUV with a Jesus fish emblem on the back. I knew I had seen it before.

As the men got closer, my stepfather yelled, "That's Phil Kleymann!"

I was excited to see him again, but I was also scared. I was so scared to talk to the guy that led me to Christ and explain to him how I was living my life. I probably had alcohol and nicotine on my breath!

It was Phil and his son, Josh. What are the odds that they would be in the same field in Iowa as us? They offered to let us walk the creek with them. Phil asked me to go with him on his side. As the small talk slowed down, he looked at me and said, "How are you doing?"

As I tried to put together some lie about how well I'm doing, he interrupted me with, "How's your spiritual life going?"

That question was the most important question that he could have asked me! As clearly as I remember that day, I can't remember if I even answered him. But the Holy Spirit changed my life that day!

My girlfriend became a believer shortly after. That year she and I decided to no longer live in sin. We got married and got involved in a local church. Brother Phil didn't know until later how much his question rocked my world, but I thank God for that cold Saturday morning in the middle of Iowa. It was over twenty years ago, but I remember it like it was yesterday. God took me back just as I was. He remains faithful.

Jerrad Wesack

My parents always taught us right from wrong and basic life lessons. My best friend Josh lived a few houses down. I spent countless hours playing at the Kleymanns. This family poured into my life. They knew Jesus. Seeds were planted into my life that took thirty or more years before they began to produce fruit. I had no idea the value of these life-giving seeds at the time. Saying grace at meal times, going to church on Sundays, and learning scriptures that I would be able to fall back on as an adult, ultimately leading me to salvation, are just a few things that this family of God taught me. I remember Phil would go into his room, shut the door to spend time with the Father and pray. These things really had an impact on my life because I did not see them anywhere else. This family would take me to church and tell me all about the good news when I was just a kid. I remember Tammy would tell me if anyone was teaching me about the Lord to make sure they showed me in the Bible.

Our families moved away, and life began to happen. As I got older, I began to experiment with drugs, and they took on a life of their own, leading me down a path of destruction for more than twenty years. They just about took my life, not to mention the stress and turmoil they caused my parents.

I was in and out of jails and prisons, fighting everyone and everything. Kaelyn and I had two children together. We were both suffering from addiction and fighting for our lives.

As I was sitting in a Covid lockdown cell in the Douglas County Jail, I picked up the Bible. I started in Revelation and read it backwards. The Lord was really getting my attention. I knew that I needed help beyond what any human could give me. I started crying out to the Lord. I had no idea what was beginning to take place. All I knew was that I hated the lies and the evil that had been surrounding me and my family. I was trying so hard to stay clean and sober and do good. I figured if I could just get it together and do good, I could live a decent life and raise and support my family. The only problem was I could not stay sober. Each relapse became increasingly worse and dangerous. I didn't understand that doing good was not the goal; the goal is life—and life comes from the Lord Jesus Christ.

The search for the truth had begun. The crucifixion of self took place over a couple of years. There were strongholds of flesh and addiction, inspired by the lies of the devil, fighting the Spirit of God, trying to drink from the Lord's cup and break bread with the devil.

> You cannot drink the cup of the Lord and the cup of demons too; you cannot have a part in both the Lord's table and the table of demons (1 Cor. 10:21 NIV).

It doesn't work!

The last time I relapsed was in June 2022. I found myself facing a twenty-five-year sentence, sitting in a twenty-three-hour lockdown cell, broken beyond words. There were no-contact orders on everyone in my family, and my business that I had just started was over. I thought I'd officially done it, lost the love of my life and my family to the evil ways of this world. This was hell on earth. I had officially come to the end of myself. I had had enough of this way of living, and I made a decision to study the word of God and find the truth. I found the truth all right, and He is a person, and his name is Jesus! And He is very much alive!

Everything I once thought and believed was being uprooted by the power of the Holy Spirit. It was a little disruptive to my old way of living, to say the least! Being in county jail is usually a terrible, terrible experience. But when you are being reintroduced to the fountain of living water and real-life disciples of Jesus Christ are bringing the message, there is no place I would rather be! I kept reading the word and meditating on it, and the discipling process started to take place in a jail cell. The Holy Spirit started showing me things about my life; He started revealing things about me and my character that were not in line with God or His kingdom. He opened my heart, and the scales fell off my eyes! He led me straight to Jesus Christ, and I accepted Him into my heart at once. I counted the cost of what it would mean to follow Him, and I made a commitment to Jesus and His kingdom. Instantly, the chains were broken, the addiction vanished, and I began to speak differently. I had been redeemed. I was saved from an eternity in hell! The old man was crucified with Christ, passing from death to life. I had been born! I was a brand-new creation in Christ! It was unbelievable! All of this happened while I was in a jail cell. The next thing I knew, the courts were releasing me to a Christian recovery program.

Things have come to pass that I couldn't even imagine. Without the divine touch of our Father, none of it would have been possible. Reconciliation of my family took place. I was able to show up to a broken relationship full of broken hearts, but I had the Kingdom of God with me. I reached out to Tammy and Phil and told them what had taken place in my life, and I asked them to come and speak to the mother of my children. She was on her deathbed from addiction. Without hesitation, they were over at my house, sharing the gospel. The power of the Holy Spirit took hold of Kaelyn with authority and led her straight to Jesus! It was amazing! A couple of weeks later, she was born again and getting baptized, and we were dedicating our children to the Kingdom of our Father! I was able to marry the love of my life, my very best friend! We came together as one in love and entered the covenant of marriage with our Triune God! As of today, we are very much involved in our church. All my charges were dismissed December 2023. We now live by the very lifeblood of another—Jesus.

Brett Henn

I grew up in a family that was considered by us, Christian. We were non-practicing Catholics. My mother, when I was very young, did tell me about Jesus and that He died for my sins, but I didn't really grasp what that meant. I attended a Catholic high school and took religion classes that never taught me about biblical salvation. It left me not believing in God one way or another. I believed that no one could really be sure, and I thought that God, if He did exist, would understand that and be happy if I just was true to what I did believe. Whatever that meant.

I graduated high school in 2001, and I met a girl that was friends with my sister. We would have conversations about God. This was the first time that I had ever heard that salvation was a gift from God and wasn't something that could be earned. Quite frankly, the idea sounded ridiculous to me. One of the first times I met her father, he sat me down on the couch and had me read the Bible with him. It was very uncomfortable.

At some point in late 2002 or early 2003, I was invited to a youth Bible study at the Kleymann's. I didn't want to attend, but I went to keep my girlfriend happy. Phil spent the first part of this study proving the accuracy of the Bible and going over all the prophecies that Jesus had fulfilled. This got my attention! I started really considering the things I had been hearing for months. I even had conversations with my sisters about end time events and where we would be spending our eternity.

At this point in time, I was very certain that Jesus was God and that He died for my sins. However, I was a fool. I thought, if my family is going to hell, then that's where I want to go. Hearing this, my girlfriend basically told me that it wasn't going to work out between us, so we broke up. A short time later, I got a call that I should go to the Kleymann's place on April 9, 2003. I don't recall the reason why I thought I was going over there, but either way it was a trick. I walked in and Tammy was sitting at the table with her Bible waiting for me. She asked me to sit down. Reluctantly, I sat.

I don't remember every detail, but I remember that it was emotional. She was asking me questions as the Spirit led her though different passages. I asked her, "Wouldn't it be easier to have faith after Jesus' death, then it would have been to have faith before his death and resurrection?"

She said, "Yes, but I know someone who is having trouble after."

She got me there! She asked if I met God right then if I would be saved. I said that I was on the verge. She turned to Romans 1:28-32 and used those verses to convict me.

She turned to John 3:16 and had me read, "For God so loved the world that he gave his one and only Son, that whoever believes in him shall not perish but have eternal life" (NIV).

Then Tammy had me read the verse again, but this time she had me personalize it. For God so loved *me* that He gave His one and only Son, that if *I* believe in Him, *I* shall not perish but have eternal life.

That was it, it felt like God had removed all other choices from me, and I was forever changed! Amen.

Eric Benson

Growing up, I dealt with a considerable amount of fear; fear of being alone, fear of health issues, and especially a fear of death. On the health front, I was nothing short of a hypochondriac when it came to medical issues, and I was convinced that some random accident or obscure medical condition was going to kill me. It seemed like every time I heard a news story about someone who had succumbed to the flu, or a football player who had suffered a collapsed lung, that the same thing would happen to me, and that it would kill me. Most of the time, I suffered in silence as I did not always tell my parents what was going on inside my mind. Though I looked like every other kid on the outside, I was often filled with anxiety and ruled by fear.

These fears continued into my teenage years and reached their climax in the summer of 1999. Fortunately, this summer would produce the cure for my fear. For the first time since I was probably seven or eight years old, I was going to Bible camp. I remember being excited to go based on my sister's experience the previous year, but for some reason I started dealing with the most intense fear I had ever experienced. Being afraid was not new to me, but something about what I was feeling and thinking about was different. I started to think about what would happen to me if I really did die? I grew up in the church and was a professed Christian, but I started to question my beliefs and where I would go if I died. This continued throughout the summer, and about two weeks before camp I remember thinking that if I could just make it to camp, I would be ok. I didn't really know why, but I believed that, and it became my goal.

Two weeks went by, and I was on my way to Willowbrook Bible Camp in Iowa with a bunch of kids and adults from my church, including Phil and Tammy Kleymann. About a half hour after we left church, I started to have thoughts about the bus going off the road and crashing before we could make it to my refuge. I'm thankful the drive was just over two hours because that was a long ride.

Even though nothing had changed when we arrived, I felt relieved, and before long I was just another crazy middle school kid having fun without a care in the world. The week went on like this, but each night we had a time of Bible study and worship together to provide me a gentle reminder that I still wasn't ok. Finally, on the last night of camp, I knew I needed to do something, as the end of our worship time was fast approaching, and nothing in my belief system had really changed. When the last song ended and the kids started heading back to their bunks, I hung around in the chapel waiting for an opportunity to pull Phil aside so we could speak without the others around. I told Phil that I was scared and that I didn't know where I would go when I died. I knew that I deserved hell, but of course I did not want to go there. Like any follower of Christ, Phil immediately took me to the Word, more specifically the Gospels. We read through a variety of passages that were all too familiar to me, and yet unknown. We read Romans 3:23, Romans 6:23, and John 3:16, probably in that order, along with many others. Phil had me place my name in those passages to make them more personal, but my mind and soul remained unchanged. I was dead, and there was nothing that could change that, until I met the Good Shepherd.

Flipping to John chapter 10, Phil asked me to close my eyes and picture the story in my mind as he read the passage to me. So, I bent over in my seat with my elbows and forearms on my legs and closed my eyes. About verse seven, I started to have a clear image in my mind of a flock following a shepherd,

> Therefore Jesus said again, "Very truly I tell you, I am the gate for the sheep. All who have come before me are thieves and robbers, but the sheep have not listened to them. I am the gate; whoever enters through me will be saved" (John 10:7-9 NIV)

As Phil continued to read, the image became clearer and started to feel more personal to me, like I was there. Then came verses 11-15:

> I am the good shepherd. The good shepherd lays down his life for the sheep. The hired hand is not the shepherd and does not own the sheep. So when he sees the wolf coming, he abandons the sheep and runs away. Then the wolf attacks the flock and scatters it. The man runs away because he is a hired hand and cares nothing for the sheep. I am the good shepherd; I know my sheep and my sheep know me—just as the Father knows me and I know the Father—and I lay down my life for the sheep. (NIV)

In those verses I found myself as a lone sheep cowering in the rocks of a hillside watching as a man was fighting off the wolves in front of me. The scene in my mind was horrible. The man was forced to the ground on his back as he was overpowered and savagely and repeatedly attacked by the wolves. I remember feeling terrified at the sight, until I met the eyes of the man. He looked at me with a love I can't describe, and in my mind, I heard him say "I did this for you." In an instant I was filled with a sense of joy and relief I can't describe. Jesus had done all of this for me! He loved me, He was never going to leave me or forsake me, and He was going to fight for me. Phil, recognizing that something had changed, as tears streamed down my cheeks, asked if I was ok, so I told him what had happened and what I had heard, and Phil asked me if I wanted to pray and thank God for what He had done. Salvation is not a feeling, but I can promise you, it can be accompanied by incredible emotion. After calling my parents and then rousing the entire camp to tell them the good news, one of my bunk mates encouraged me to run some laps around the pool outside our cabin to run off some energy. I will never forget that night, my Shepherd, or the man God used to lead me to faith!

In the many years since I met Jesus, I have had seasons of following and times of wandering. I have grown in my knowledge and understanding of the Truth, and I have been tested on many occasions with varying degrees of successes and failures in response. When I have followed, He has taken me further than I could have imagined. When I have wandered, He has never let me go too far, and He has always brought me back to the narrow path. When I have been afraid, He has reassured me. When I have felt alone, He has reminded me that He is with me. Why? Because my Lord is faithful. Before I ever drew a breath, I was known to Him, and He who began a good work in me will finish it!

Mike Matulka

I was raised in a Catholic family, with the older, rigid Catholic beliefs. Religion and God were pretty much forced upon me at an early age. I hated anything that had to do with religion. When I reached driving age, my sister and I would opt to go to the early mass. But instead of sitting through the service, we would simply go to the church, grab that week's bulletin, then just drive around for an hour or so. When it was about the time mass would end, we would go home and present the bulletin like we'd been there. That's just one example of many tricks we would use to avoid God things.

When I went off to college, God was the last thing on my mind. It was obvious that I was living only for myself. Every now and then I would run into folks that were believers, and for the most part, they were cool people. But that was for them, not for me.

Close to the end of my first year of college, I met a girl who was different than any other girl I had met previously. Instantly, I was attracted to her, and I knew that I was going to pursue her, and I did, but I knew I couldn't approach her the same

Josh

way I did other girls. I was prepared to slow roll this pursuit. So we started off for a good while as just friends, hanging out and going out with other friends. We did this for so long that I was getting very antsy because it was not moving as quickly as I wanted it to. One evening, I mustered up the courage to officially ask her to date me. But she answered in a way that totally shocked me. She said "Mike, I do want to date you, but there is someone I love more."

You can probably imagine everything that was going through my head, "Who is he? Where is he?"

She said, "No Mike, I love God the most, and He holds the first place in my life. And as much as I want to, I can't date you because you are not a believer."

I tried to keep it cool on the outside, but on the inside, I was screaming "NOOOOO, not her!!! She can't be one of those!" Mind you, I did know that she was a believer, but not *that kind* of believer—more on the level of just being a good person. I never would've thought or imagined that God could be that real in someone's life. So, I had a decision to make. Do I call this all off and just move on? But I really, really liked her. Do I attempt to find out what this version of God is all about?

I chose to cautiously investigate. I knew what I knew about God at the time, but I didn't know what she knew. And it seemed to be a night and day difference. So I found myself going to church, youth groups, and even Bible camp—anything she was going to, I was going there too.

After a while of being immersed into this new culture and new concept of what God could be to me, my heart began to soften. But there was this constant inner battle. Did I really want to give up my life and all that I have right now for this unknown God thing? It may be working for them, but I'm still not sure it's for me.

One evening at youth group, I was really struggling. It was a fun evening with friends and there was an awesome message, but there was a raging battle inside me. Both Tammy and Phil sniffed it out by simply asking me questions. We ended up sitting all together on the couch in their living room, and Phil started walking me through some Bible verses to read. This was really good, and each verse he pointed to was, one by one, canceling my doubts. I wanted to believe, but I just couldn't get past, "How do you know that you're saved and can spend the rest of eternity in Heaven after you pass from this earth?"

Phil and Tammy had me read 1 John 5:13, "I write these things to you who believe in the name of the Son of God so that you may KNOW that you have eternal life" (NIV).

At that moment all the walls came tumbling down. I knew in my heart that I was saved, and I confessed with my mouth that He is Lord of my life. Wow! what a life-changing, life-giving moment—Hallelujah!

After that, I kept going to church, youth groups, and yes, even Bible camps. And I was now dating you-know-who! But I would be remiss to tell you that after I got saved, everything was perfect and that I was perfect. Yes, everything was squared up in the spiritual, but for that to manifest in the natural, would prove to be a lifelong journey. I was a newborn, with all the baggage of my past. So, not only do I have a lot to learn, but God is working on healing all these areas of my life. At least now I'm not in this alone through the process.

All this takes time to work through, and I didn't do everything right, especially when it came to relationships. Past addictions to pornography, that weren't conquered and healed yet, tainted, and eventually severed, my dating relationship. Through the guilt and shame of that particular sin, and me trying to cover it up, I broke the trust and hurt a lot of people close to me. I truly apologize to all of those I hurt due to my ignorance.

Guilt and shame are the primary weapons the enemy uses to keep you bound by sin and challenge your worthiness of a Savior. The amazing thing is that our loving Father doesn't look

Josh

to our sin, but He looks to His Son and the price He paid for my sin. The two greatest words in the human language are, NOT GUILTY!

Fast-forward twenty years, I now have a wife and three sons. We are quite involved at our local church. Life is pretty good, and I consider myself blessed. My hope is that, in return, I'm a blessing to the folks around me.

Of course, I could keep going on and on with story after story about both successes and challenges I've had over the years, but the one thing I can tell you is, since that day sitting on the couch in Phil and Tammy's living room, God has been with me and for me every day since.

A big thank you to Phil & Tammy Kleymann for your unwavering obedience to the call of God! It has impacted so many lives, I am just one of many! Blessings to you and to all reading this!

For what thanks can we render to God again for you, for all the joy wherewith we joy for your sakes before our God.
—1 Thessalonians 3:9

CHAPTER 17

Josh

"I love it at your house. It's so peaceful here!" The neighborhood kids came to the Kleymann's house for kid's club or just to hang out with Phil and Tammy's kids. They envied the love and structure of the Kleymann home. Some parents mocked Phil and Tammy for their vocal religion, yet they were glad to let the kids play at their house.

Phil and Tammy had two children, first a rambunctious boy and a little later, a beautiful girl. Tammy's whole life had revolved around giving her children a better upbringing than she had had. She studiously avoided the example her parents had given her. She turned to godly role models in the church and read Christian parenting books. Phil provided stability. He was present as a father to the children, though he had a busy schedule with work and church.

Despite these advantages, there is no perfection under the sun. Each person must exercise their own free will as to whether he will trust in the goodness of God, regardless of circumstances. Just as Tammy didn't have to be a slave to her horrifying past, so her children weren't forced to a predestined outcome by their upbringing. They had advantages, no doubt, but every circumstance has its pitfalls. Josh fell into one of these.

Josh saw the power of the Spirit of God manifested in his parents' lives. He saw answered prayer, and he watched them win young people to Christ. He saw their humanity, too, but their faults did not obscure his conviction of the truth of the gospel. As far back as he can remember, he knew God was real and the gospel was true.

Josh took his privileged position in a Christian family for granted. He memorized Scripture and embraced the truth of the biblical principles his parents taught, but he did not experience the power of a changed life. When he was around seven years old, he was frightened about where he would spend eternity. He found his mom and told her about his fears. Without pressuring him, Tammy shared some verses with him and told him to be honest with God. The next morning he told her, "I talked to the Lord, and I'm saved now." Tammy was hopeful. This is what a believing mother wants to hear from her children, but she neither encouraged nor discouraged this profession.

Josh had believed the facts of the gospel and had gone through the motions that seemed right to him. He had clear head knowledge about Christ, but he confused that for faith. When doubts plagued him, as they often did, he silenced them by assuring himself that he was OK. His pride was attached to this childhood profession, and he couldn't let go of it. He was the preacher's kid. Deep down he knew he wasn't saved, but he blocked out the pings of conscience. He told himself, "You believe, so just be quiet." He couldn't admit that he didn't have peace with God.

Josh went to a Christian school through eighth grade. He hung out with other kids from Christian families and easily maintained his profession of Christianity. When his parents felt a financial pinch, they decided to send Josh to the public high school.

Public School

The moral filth in the public high school shocked Josh. The first week he was there, he went to the principle and said, "Call my mom and tell her to get me out of here!"

The principle, Mr. Bell, was a Christian man. He asked Josh, "Where is it harder to walk and exercise your faith, at the Christian school where you were or here?"

"Here."

"Where would God be most pleased with you?"

"Here."

Mr. Bell reached in his pocket and pulled out a carved cross. He gave it to Josh and told him to keep it in his pocket. "When you feel the cross in your pocket, pray for me, and I will pray for you."

This well-meant support may perhaps have been enough to keep Josh if he had had the indwelling power of the Holy Spirit. He did not.

During his ninth-grade year, Josh participated in the Fellowship of Christian Athletes and made friends with moral kids. The next year, as he got into skateboarding, his friends were more worldly-minded. By his junior year, the friends Josh hung out with were experimenting with alcohol, and Josh went to the parties. At first, he would not drink, but this put him in a dangerous position. Getting the Christian kid to drink a beer became an exciting challenge for his friends.

Soon, while at a big party, a guy stuck a beer in Josh's face. He drank it. It was amazing. He loved it, and he started on a downward spiral. Before long he tried a joint of marijuana in a similar circumstance.

Over the summer between his junior and senior years, Josh was getting high every weekend. Once school started, he smoked weed every day before school and did other drugs whenever he could. He was still going to church and youth group. He was

Josh

outgoing and talented, and he became very good at living a double life.

Both parents worked. His mom worked at the same restaurant where Josh did. She got off her shift when he came on. He waved at her and said, "I love you, Mom," as she left work, and she didn't suspect that he was high. She and Phil were disappointed that Josh hadn't shown as much interest in the Word of God as they thought a Christian should, but it hadn't raised enough concern for them to wonder if he knew the Lord. They trusted him and trusted his profession of salvation.

Josh graduated from high school in 2000. That summer his parents went to Colorado for a camp. Josh and his younger sister stayed home. While the parents were gone, Josh went to a huge house party. The cops came, and Josh got busted. He was ticketed for *minor in possession*. His cover was blown, and he didn't know what to do.

One of the friends who was at the party was headed to Wyoming. He said to Josh, "I can't afford this ticket. I'm headed back to Cheyenne. Want to come with me? They have great drugs there." This seemed at the time like Josh's way out. He packed a bag, grabbed his graduation money, and took off in the middle of the night.

When Josh's sister saw what was happening, she called her parents and told them. Phil was just about to give a message at camp when the director called Tammy to the phone for an emergency call. It was her daughter, "Josh is going to Wyoming. He was at a party and got a ticket for possession of alcohol."

Tammy was in shock. Because of her past drug use, she had prided herself that she would know if one of her kids was using. That self-deception was pulled out from under her. Concern for her son's eternal well-being would not allow a new form of pride to take control. She wouldn't keep this a secret. She was going to enlist the prayers of everyone she knew! She and Phil came home from camp, but not before asking for prayer for their wayward son. The request went out to Christians around the country as the campers and workers returned to their homes.

Tammy wanted to immediately go to Wyoming to find Josh, but Phil was adamant: Let the prodigal go. Josh had done exactly what the prodigal son had done, and they needed to respond according to the biblical example. They had to wait for him to come to his senses and return, as the father did in the parable of the prodigal son (Lk. 15:11-32). Tammy's heart wanted to run after him, but she knew that Phil was right. Just pray.

Wyoming

While he was in Omaha, Josh's family and church had provided him with a wall of restraint. Now that he was away from home, all moral discipline was loosed. There was no more double life and nothing to keep him from the expression of his sinful passions. He lived among drug dealers, helped to run drugs across state boarders, and he gave no thought to anything but getting high. He attended rave parties where he did mixed drugs and stayed high for days at a time.

A friend of Josh's called Phil and Tammy to tell them that he had been on a three-day high with crack, crank, and ecstasy. Tammy could barely take it in, but even in this, the Lord was her strength. God had provided friends from around the country who understood and supported her and Phil during this trying time. It only lasted two or three months, but what an intense few months it was!

Josh, by nature, is a person of extremes. Whatever he does, he does to the fullest. He was also a reckless teenager. When challenged to drink an entire bottle of whiskey in one chug, he did it. Afterward he collapsed on a street corner. But for an angel who called 911, he would have died. He was taken to emergency services and woke up the next day in jail.

Phil and Tammy got the ER bill. Josh had had an insurance card in his wallet. They knew he was alive. It was poor comfort, but God was hearing their cries.

Tammy called the hospital to find out what had happened. Because of HIPAA, the hospital staff wouldn't tell her anything. She told them, if she couldn't know, she was not going to pay. She took Josh off the insurance.

Teary-eyed, Tammy called the ambulance and begged for information. The woman who answered was a mother. She poured affection on Tammy and tried to comfort her. She also told her that Josh had been treated for alcohol poisoning.

Answered Prayer

On October 12, 2000, Josh woke up in a crack house. He had been sleeping on the couch. A guy in a chair across the room turned on the TV. There was war between Israel and Palestine. Josh was startled by the news. He had heard about the second coming of the Lord all through his childhood. He knew that Jerusalem would become a cup of trembling in the last days. The next piece of news was the bombing of the U.S.S. Cole off the coast of Yemen. Josh was terrified. He feared that he would next hear about Christians disappearing in the rapture. He needed to get away from the TV and get his mind off this stuff.

Josh got up and went to the kitchen. He started washing dishes, but instead of telling his conscience to be quiet like he usually did, he started talking to God. He had been raised in a spiritual bubble, but he looked at his life and saw that he was in bad shape. To God he said, "The gospel is supposed to be so simple that a child can understand it. Why is it so hard for me?"

Josh thought of calling his parents to ask them how he could be saved. That wouldn't do. He had run out on them and hadn't talked to them in a couple months. He thought about some of his Christian friends. The same thing. Then a memory verse from AWANA popped into his mind.

> Ask, and it shall be given you; seek, and ye shall find; knock, and it shall be opened unto you (Matt. 7:7).

Josh heard a voice inside his head say, "You don't need to talk to your parents or your friends. You need to talk to Me."

Josh had no pride left. He saw the drug-running punk that he was. He expected the rapture any moment, and all he wanted was to be saved. He called out to God, "The gospel is so simple, but in my pride, I missed it. I want to see. You have to show me."

In that moment something clicked. The head knowledge became real. Josh reached out like Blind Bartimaeus and laid his eyes on the Lord Jesus Christ.

Josh went back to the living room and sat down on the couch. The TV was still playing. The news no longer terrified him. He listened with a strange peace in his heart.

On the coffee table in front of him was his bag of weed and a pack of cigarettes. He looked at them, and a voice in his head said, "You don't want them anymore." Something had radically changed.

Even more surprising were the words that came out of his mouth. He had been using the foul language that naturally accompanies the profane drug culture he had embraced. He started talking to the other guy in the room, and without any effort on his part, the four-letter words were gone.

James says no man can tame the tongue (James 3:8). The instantaneous taming of Josh's tongue could only be the work of the Spirit of God. Josh leaned back and exclaimed to himself, "I just got saved." For the first time in his life he had absolute assurance.

Josh didn't have a telephone. He ran down the street to a friend's and placed a collect call. His mom answered the phone. He told her, "I have good news." Tammy was skeptical. What

Josh

good news could he have? The last she had heard he was mixing hard drugs. Nonetheless, she was glad to hear from him. She told him to hang up, and she would call him back.

"Mom, I just got saved!"

Well, that was good news! They talked for 45 minutes. Phil got on the phone, too. He asked Josh what he wanted to do.

"I want to come home."

"When?"

"Tonight."

Phil contacted the bussing system and purchased Josh a ticket to leave Cheyenne at 1:00 a.m. Tammy picked him up at the bus station in Omaha the next morning.

Within a few days of his return to Omaha, Josh attended a church event where he was asked to give his testimony. Afterward, Dale Gleason[4] pulled him aside and asked, "October 12, huh? What time?"

"Probably around 9:00 in the morning."

"Let me tell you the rest of the story," said Dale. On October 12, Dale was at a meeting of elders and church workers in Connecticut. There were around two hundred Christian leaders in attendance. At 11:00 a.m. Eastern Time, they gathered for an hour of prayer before lunch. Dale went up front and wrote Josh's name on the white board. At the very same time that God was dealing with Josh in a crack house in Wyoming, two hundred Christians were praying for him in Connecticut.

Starting Over

The first year after he was saved, Josh was on fire for the Lord. The Bible had come alive for him, and he wasn't interested in anything else. He loved hearing from God as he read the pages of Scripture. He took to heart truths that had never resonated in the same way, though he had heard them before. He spoke boldly about the beauties of Christ, and he was used of God in the lives of others.

The following year, Josh went to Bible School in Iowa. While there, just a little more than a year after his conversion, he participated in a childish prank that, in the providence of God, was blown way out of proportion. He and some friends snatched bags of Halloween candy out of the hands of some teenage kids, intending to return them immediately. Instead, they were detained until the police arrived and arrested them for stealing. The story of kids from a Christian college stealing Halloween candy was painted in the worst possible light and taken up by the press around the country. With all the negative publicity, the college staff felt themselves pressured into a corner. To save face, they expelled Josh.

Phil and Tammy heard the nation-wide news story that some kids from a Christian college had been arrested for stealing candy. Later in the day, they got a phone call from a friend. He asked if they had heard the story. "Yeah, we heard," said Phil.

"That was Josh."

Phil took it in stride. When he got the chance, he explained to Josh, "My friends and I should have been in jail for the things we did at your age, but we weren't professing Christians. You've got to watch yourself. You can't spit on the sidewalk without the devil making it a case against you. What else do you think was going on in Iowa that night? But a childish prank is making the news because you profess Christ. You need to double down and be careful."

Being kicked out of Bible school was humiliating for Josh, but going back the next semester was probably worse. His reputation, already tarnished by his indulgence in the drug culture, was brought even lower by his rash prank. But God knew what Josh needed, and the self-righteous platitudes of students and teachers, though angering, were also useful to keep him from putting confidence in himself.

After his short stint at Bible school, Josh enrolled in flight school with a plan to be a pilot. He had been warned that being a pilot was no job for a married man. That wasn't a problem. He planned to stay single. Until he met Joanna.

Joanna

In July 2003, Phil and Tammy were going to Storybook Lodge Christian Camp, a Bible camp in northern Minnesota. They heard that the camp was short on male counselors, so they urged Josh to take a week off from his construction job and go with them. He did so.

Joanna Bulow was working in the kitchen. She had been raised in a godly family and had learned to trust the Lord for salvation and spiritual growth. The desire of her heart was to serve God and do His will.[5]

As soon as Josh saw Joanna, he felt a tugging at his heart. This was to be his wife! He didn't have time to get to know her during camp, but he felt a strong conviction that he ought to pursue her, so he sent her an email. He persuaded her first to talk, then to date, then to marry him in November, 2004.

The Lord providentially led Josh and Joanna to St. Louis, Missouri, in answer to the prayers of Joanna's mother. She believed it would be best for them to start their life together in a fresh location, away from both families. Josh started a floor tiling business in St. Louis and was quite successful until the housing market turned in 2010. Joanna worked in a financial office. She was valued there, and when business slowed for Josh, her income helped them continue to make ends meet without much change in lifestyle. Then Joanna got pregnant.

Josh didn't have strong convictions about having his wife stay home with the children, but he knew it was important to Joanna and her family. He wanted to honor their convictions. In order to provide sufficiently for Joanna to leave her job, he would have to abandon his failing business. He put in applications for jobs all over St. Louis. Nothing came up.

North Dakota

Joanna's dad did construction work in Minot, North Dakota. The 2011 flood, on the heels of an oil boom from the previous decade, had created a severe housing shortage and a scarcity of construction workers. A large housing project had landed in Al Bulow's lap. He called Josh and asked if he would be willing to come up and help with the flooring.

It was hard to leave the church in St. Louis. It had been on its last dying leg when Josh and Joanna had arrived. Their young enthusiasm had helped to breathe life into it. Now, the elders of the church were aging or leaving, and Josh worried what would happen to the church when he left. One of the brothers assured him, "It's not your church." The Lord raised up new workers when Josh left, and it continues to be a healthy, thriving church.

Josh and Joanna and their newborn son moved to North Dakota. Josh soon found more work than he knew what to do with. The Lord blessed his commitment to family, and his income more than amply replaced what was lost from Joanna staying at home with their son.

In Minot, the Kleymanns were involved in a small but healthy church. Josh and Joanna were faithful there, but they were able to take the sidelines more than they had in Missouri. With two more children and a booming business, it was natural that they did so, especially given Josh's all-or-nothing personality.

One morning he woke up realizing that he was a slave to the American Dream. He was making a lot of money, but what was it worth? His nice house and two-car garage filled with toys were of no eternal value. He went weeks without cracking a Bible. He was burnt out on business. The pressure of building high-end homes for people whose whole perspective seemed to begin and end with material things destroyed his job satisfaction. He started applying for work that would relieve him of the responsibility of owning and running a business.

Joanna's brother had moved the family construction business to Valley City, North Dakota. When he found out that Josh was looking for a change, he invited Josh to join him. The pace in Valley City would be more relaxed, and the job would be less physically demanding. He would be doing general construction, rather than getting on his knees to do flooring. Josh bought into ACB Construction, going half and half with his brother-in-law. He moved his family to Valley City in 2015.

With his intense and passionate personality, Josh once again threw himself into his work. He is not one of the few who are gifted to manage the demands of business and maintain a strong spiritual walk as well. No man can have two masters, and each time Josh started a business, it became his master. Though sharing responsibility with his brother-in-law, Josh was consumed with his work. He had no time or energy to take any responsibility in the church he attended.

Josh was dissatisfied with his life. He was consumed with the things of earth, still chasing the American Dream. When he was able to get away from work, he threw himself into hunting and fishing. He had lost the joy of his first love for Christ. He rarely opened his Bible, and he had no prayer life. He convinced himself that this was normal Christianity, but he was inwardly discontent.

2020

In 2019, despite Josh's commitment to it, the construction business was struggling. New Year's morning 2020, a wind blew down sixty-thousand-dollars' worth of newly installed trusses. Josh had nightmares about not being able to meet payroll. He believed the business problems to be the chastening of the Lord. He had planned to escape the burdens of business and give himself more to the Lord, but he had not done so. Now he wanted out. Life was unbearable for him to the point that he began to fantasize about death.

One evening he confessed to Joanna, "I've been saved twenty years. I've squandered it. I've been living for my own vain pursuits. The dagger in my heart is remembering the fire of my first love. The passion and hunger for the Lord I used to have as I watched the Lord transform me and use me. I want that back."

As he spoke to his wife, Josh spoke to the Lord as well. He heard the Lord speak to him by an inner voice, asking, "What do you want?"

"I want my first love back."

Instantly, something happened. It was like a second birth. Something changed that was, from Josh's perspective, as radical as his salvation experience had been. The next day he got up and read his Bible. He started getting up earlier and earlier to spend time in the Scriptures. God began speaking to him, causing his heart to burn once again. This experience suddenly and drastically changed the course of his life. He heard the Lord's call to *leave his net in the boat* (Matt. 4:20) and devote himself completely to the work of God. His brother-in-law continued to run ACB Construction, but Josh was out.

Israel

As he sought the Lord about how best to serve Him, Josh became convinced that he ought to go to Israel. In 2022, he made a month's trip to the Jewish homeland. He had heard that Israel was a depressing place to share the gospel, but he found that God has begun to prepare the hearts of His people. Josh had numerous opportunities to speak to people about the beauties of Christ

Jesus. While there, a woman assumed him to be Jewish. Josh said he wasn't, but he loved the Jewish people.

"Why do you have a Jewish name?" she asked.

Josh had been unaware that *Kleymann* was Jewish. He has since discovered that he does have Jewish ancestry, and that some of his Kleymann forebears suffered in the Holocaust. If he can substantiate his Jewish roots to the satisfaction of the nation, he will immigrate to Israel and become one of the many Jews to return to the land, or *make Aliyah*.

Remember therefore from whence thou art fallen, and repent, and do the first works. —Revelation 2:5

CHAPTER 18

The Choice to Serve

Phil's lifelong dream of owning land in the country had come true. In 2003, he bought twelve beautiful acres in a valley outside Omaha.

Phil and Tammy used their place in the country for the Lord's work. They had weekly young people's groups and occasionally held weekend camps when they brought kids from the inner city out to their acreage. Besides chalk talks, they offered horse riding, hay rack rides, shooting a BB gun, sleeping in tents, and other activities. Phil wanted the city kids to have a chance to fish. There was a stream on the property, but the banks were steep and dangerous, and there was no good place to enter the creek. Phil had put "fishing" on the flyer for their first retreat, but they didn't know how they were going to make it work.

A Fishing Hole

While at a nearby auction, Phil and Tammy bid on an apple picker. In the bundle with the apple picker was a fishing spear. They had no use for the spear, so when a young man asked for it, they gave it to him. This led to a conversation with his parents who turned out to be neighbors who had a pond on their property. Out of gratitude for the fishing spear, the neighbors said to Phil and Tammy, "If there's ever anything we can do for you, let us know."

On the way home, Phil and Tammy had an idea. The next day, they went over to the neighbors, explained to them that they were having a weekend Christian camp, and asked, "Can we bring kids over to fish?"

The couple looked at each other, and their eyes got big. "We have been praying that God would use our property! Our kids are grown and gone. We would love you to bring kids over, but on one condition: You let us help." Thus, in answer to the desire of their hearts, fishing became a part of the experience at the weekend camps that Phil and Tammy conducted for about ten years.

In 2006 the trucking company Phil worked for was sold. Phil lost the seniority that he had gained by working for the same company for eighteen years. He found another job that accommodated his summer schedule fairly well and allowed him some vacation time to go to Bible camps. When that company was bought by another trucking outfit, however, he became the twenty-second guy in line for vacations. Summer camp work came to a screeching halt. Josh offered to support him through the summer, so Phil and Tammy could spend the whole season going from camp to camp, preaching the gospel, and doing chalk talks, but Phil had to refuse. He couldn't take the whole summer off and expect to have a job in the fall.

Earthly Kingdom

Phil loved his place on the bluff. No neighbors were visible from his house. He had fields and fences; cliffs and creeks; horses, goats, and other farm animals; not to mention the abundant wildlife that wandered the land. He could sit on the porch and hear a stream babbling in the yard. He could hunt in his backyard.

One day when Phil was in the deer stand on the bluff behind his house, he looked over his earthly kingdom and gazed at his beautiful property. He realized that it didn't satisfy. God had allowed him to have it for a season that he might experience firsthand that even the good things of earth do not fulfill. He had had more satisfaction with a simpler life when he had more time to do the Lord's work.

Years previously Phil had started out on an adventure with God, and he couldn't continue on that path with his feet so deeply planted in the earth. "Does this look like the place where a pilgrim lives?" he thought. "It doesn't look like the tent of Abraham. It looks like the property of someone who is planning on staying for a while."

Phil realized that he had a choice. He could keep his place in the country and move quietly into old age, or he could let it go. If he stayed on the property, he was pinned to it. Other than the mini-camps that he held on the property, there would be no camp work. Both he and Tammy had to work long hours to keep it, and he couldn't get time off in the summer. He decided to let it go.

Tammy agreed. She loved the big house and the opportunities it provided for hospitality, but gospel work was vastly more important. With her testimony, she had the keys to unlock doors to hurting kids. Her openness about her childhood experiences gives young people confidence to talk to her and reveal the hurts that they have experienced. This gives her a unique opportunity to share the love of Christ. She missed doing this on a larger scale.

As Phil and Tammy were pondering these things, Josh called. He had been praying that his parents would get back into camp work, and he had a plan. Josh and his brother-in-law Aaron were purchasing a snowplowing business. They invited Phil to join them. He would work primarily in the winter, and do a little construction work with them when he wanted. All summer, he and Tammy would be free to do camp work.

In 2016 Phil and Tammy moved to Valley City, North Dakota. They traded their beautiful, large house with twelve acres and all their animals for a modest duplex shared with their son and his family on a crowded street of a small town.

Tim Yokom

Phil plowed snow in the winter. In the spring and fall, and when he wasn't at camp in the summer, he worked at ACB Construction. Tim Yokom also worked for ACB.

Tim had been a hard-working, hard-partying house builder for many years. As a comparatively young man, he had quit drinking, but meth use filled him with paranoia and severely affected his family life. In 2004, Tim had health problems and intense pain that drove him to his knees, but having no hope in Christ, his prayer was to die. God graciously did not answer this prayer. Because of his health concerns, Tim quit smoking and drugs. Nonetheless, something was obviously missing in his life. He felt angry all the time, and he had a very short fuse.

Around 2017, when the company Tim had worked for went under, ACB took him on. The first few days at work, Tim wasn't sure what to make of the Christian conversation before and during work. He wondered how he was going to fit in. Phil and some of the other guys liked to play "Stump the Chump," a game of asking one another tough Bible questions. Tim listened.

The more Tim listened to the men talk about God and the Bible, the more interested he got. He asked questions and started praying and reading the Bible for himself. Intellectually, he believed that Jesus had died for him, but he wondered, "Does that mean I'm saved?" He confided his uncertainty to Phil.

In July 2020, Tim went camping with the families of the men from ACB. He was discouraged. He didn't know whether or not he was saved, and he didn't know how to find out. On the camping trip, the families treated Tim like he was one of their own. On Sunday, July 12, they held a Sunday service at the campground. There was singing and Bible reading. One of the men read Luke 7. The chapter is about a sinful woman who washed Jesus' feet, but Tim was day dreaming. He was in his own world, staring into the trees, watching the wind blow. He heard only the last line, "Your faith has saved you. Go in peace" (Lk. 7:50 NKJV).

This word from God pierced his heart and answered his question. In an instant, his understanding of the gospel was no longer merely intellectual assent. His heart was filled with confidence in God's goodness. Tim says, "An incredible calm came over me. All my worries went away." After the service, he turned to Josh and told him what happened. They rejoiced together and Tim broke down in tears of relief. His life changed completely from that day forward.

> He also brought me up out of a horrible pit, Out of the miry clay, And set my feet upon a rock, And established my steps. He has put a new song in my mouth—Praise to our God (Ps. 40:2-3 NKJV).

Motorhome

For ease of traveling and for a place to stay while at camps and in between them, Phil and Tammy decided to buy a motorhome. They looked online, made phone calls, and drove around the state. Shortly before a trip to Hidden Acres in Iowa, Tammy found a dealership in Pierre, South Dakota, with a motorhome for sale. She asked Phil to stop there on the way to Iowa.

"It's not on the way. We would have to go west as well as south to get there."

Tammy was adamant. She wanted to look at that motorhome. She was so insistent that Phil gave in. He called the place and made arrangements to look at it on a Saturday morning.

The motorhome had some water damage and wasn't what Phil and Tammy were looking for. The young man who showed it to them suggested that since they had come so far to see it, they should take it for a test drive.

"Sure," said Phil, "we can do that."

The salesman asked them where they had come from and where they were going.

"We drove down from North Dakota. We are on our way to Iowa where we will be speaking at a Bible camp. I share the good news of Jesus Christ with young people and old people."

The man was silent for a while then said, "Can I share something with you?"

"Sure."

"I have the best job in this company. I make good money. I have a big house, a boat house, and more toys than most people. I'm telling you this so you will understand, I have all these things, but I have a big hole in my heart. Something is missing."

Tammy jumped on it. "Do you know what's missing? It's a relationship with your Creator."

Phil nearly drove the big motorhome off the road.

Tammy asked, "Jason, how can we know we have peace with God?" As Phil drove back to the dealership, Tammy took Jason through the Scriptures, showing him the gospel of salvation as laid out in the Bible. He was all ears. They talked for hours in the parking lot. Phil watched as Jason broke down in tears, professed faith, and then lightened up.

Jason told them that he had a friend who had been inviting him to church. A week or so previously he had gone to church and heard the same things that Phil and Tammy were telling him. He talked to a church counselor afterward, and they talked about some of the same things Tammy was talking about, but he hadn't fully received it. As he got up to leave, the counselor said to him, "Jason, I want you to know, God is going to send someone to see you."

Jason said to Phil and Tammy, "I guess you're them."

"I guess we are," said Phil.

"Thank you," said Jason. He keeps in touch with Phil and Tammy, and he goes to his friend's church.

The Kleymanns later found a 1995 diesel powered motorhome. It hasn't exactly been trouble-free, but it has been a great blessing nonetheless. Using the motorhome means they don't have to pack and unpack as many times. It gives them a place to stay at the smaller camps, and it allows for their dog, Jimmy, to go along. Despite the troubles that are sure to arise when traveling in an older motorhome, the Lord has always been faithful to provide for them and to turn their trials to blessings. Sometimes providential miracles sustain them as they travel. Other times their plans are changed in ways that God uses for good.

Bible Study

When Phil and Tammy moved to Valley City, they got involved in the community and the local church. In 2019, Phil, Josh, and other men from their church prayed together about ways to make an impact on the town for the gospel of Jesus Christ. They prayed, "We want to be relevant. Show us how to reach the town."

Josh started getting together with a young man for Bible study. Phil joined them, and others wanted to come. Because of their jobs, they requested that the study be held in the evenings. Phil approached the owner of a coffee shop called Alley Beans and asked if they could use the shop for Bible study.

"That's why we started this business. We want to serve the Lord with it," the owner told him. "What time do you want to have your study?"

"After 6:00."

"We close at 6:00, but we will leave the store open for you."

The store put coffee out for the Bible study guys, leaving a tip jar for free-will offerings. Men from around town started attending the study. Lots of guys come and go. Some have been impacted with the gospel. Others have grown in faith. Often there are fifteen to twenty men present, including the shop owner when he can come. Anyone can speak and ask questions, and the men dig deep into the Word of God.

Dearly beloved, I beseech you as strangers and pilgrims, abstain from fleshly lusts, which war against the soul.
—1 Peter 2:11

CHAPTER 19

Tim Van Hal

"God sent Phil and Tammy to Valley City for me." This is Tim Van Hal's strong conviction. He had lived for years with a terrifying consciousness that he was not right with God, but he had not dared to confide in anyone about it, until he met Phil.

Tim had been raised by believing parents who took him to a gospel-preaching church. When he was ten years old, he was deeply concerned about his soul and told his dad that he wanted to be saved. They talked for an hour about truths he thought he already knew, but in the end, he still didn't understand how to be saved. He left that conversation without any peace in his soul, and he didn't bring it up with his dad again, though his conscience nagged him. When he was overcome with fear, he would think about God for a day or two. Then he would do whatever he could to get his mind off spiritual things and relieve the pressure.

When he left the family home, he avoided church. He tried drinking, and he married a party girl. Alcohol never drowned out his conscience, so he quit using it. His wife, however, continued the party lifestyle. After eight years of marriage, Tim found out that she was cheating on him with a trusted friend. His world went out from under him. He was in Montana attending a horse-shoeing school at the time. Devastated, he decided to go to church. He went to a little store-front Baptist church where he heard hell-fire and brimstone and a solid gospel appeal. He got out as fast as he could.

False Conversion

Tim went to his camper and wept, overwhelmed with a desire for his life to be different. He drove back to town to talk to the pastor. The pastor asked, "Do you believe that Jesus died for your sins?"

"Of course I do," said Tim. "I believe everything in the Bible."

The pastor pronounced him saved.

Tim remonstrated, saying he had no peace.

"That will come," the pastor said. "Call your parents and tell them you have been saved."

Tim called his parents. They were ecstatic. But the peace never came. He had no real repentance and no true faith. Within a few days, Tim knew that he hadn't been saved. Nothing had changed. He had no more fruit in his life than before, and he had just as much fear of judgment. But now he had one more obstacle bolstering his pride and keeping him from open confession of the truth. He had made a proclamation of salvation. He could not go back on it. When he returned to Valley City, he started attending his parents' church, not mentioning that he had never been baptized.

Every day Tim thought about the fact that he was going to hell, but he told himself he had done everything he could and tried to brush it off.

After his divorce, Tim met Debby, a Christian woman who had also been recently divorced. Tim convinced her that he was a Christian, and they got married in 1993.

Tim was more active in conservative politics than in spiritual concerns. Knowing that his conversion had been false, he did not want to go to his parents' church where it could be exposed. Eventually he and Debby started going to a prominent Baptist church. Tim busied himself with social issues and tried not to think about the state of his own soul.

Conviction of Sin

Tim met Phil and Tammy at a political event. They quickly became friends, and Phil invited Tim to the men's Bible study at the coffee shop. Tim didn't want to go, but to keep up appearances, he said he would.

At the Bible study, Tim heard things that had never registered with him before. Primarily, Tim realized that, in his current state, he was an enemy of God. The first step for him to be able to understand and receive the gospel was to have a deep conviction of his need for it and to truly believe his position as a sinner before God.

In 2020, Josh and Tammy posted frequently on Facebook about the soon-coming rapture of the church. When Tim saw these posts, his blood would run cold. He could not read what they had to say. Nonetheless, thoughts about the coming of the Lord and the condition of his own soul began to bother him more and more until he was in a state of deep misery. He was not able to shake off his distress like he had in the past. He thought about it all day every day. Noticing how quiet and moody he was, Debby asked him what was wrong.

Tim knew very well what was wrong, but he said, "Nothing."

One morning, having been in agony for nearly two months, Tim went downtown to open his laundromat. His friend Terry came in and found him in tears. "Will you do me a favor?" Tim asked. "I've got a problem. Will you pray for me?"

Tim didn't tell him what his problem was, and Terry didn't pry. He got on his knees in the laundromat and prayed for God to bless Tim and grant a solution to his problem.

When Tim left the laundromat, instead of going directly home, he decided to drive by Phil's house. "If he's outside, I'll talk to him," he thought. Phil wasn't outside, but the light was on, and Tim could see the top of Phil's head as he sat in his reading chair by the window. Tim drove by the house, then stopped and called. Phil invited him over for coffee.

When Tim came in, Phil and Tammy could see that he was distressed. He blurted out, "I'm not saved. I'm 67. I've been going to church my whole life, but I still don't understand it."

Phil and Tammy were stunned. They had never suspected that Tim wasn't saved.

When Tim sat down, Phil's typically aloof lap dog, Jimmy, jumped up in Tim's lap and looked sympathetically into Tim's sobbing face.

Phil opened his Bible and went over the same truths that Tim had heard many times. They talked for over two hours. Debby was expecting him home to help with canning. She called and asked where he was.

"At Phil's."

"What are you doing there?"

"Having a Bible study."

Now that was an odd thing for Tim to be doing! Debby knew about his moodiness, but she was completely unaware of the turmoil going on his heart.

Before Tim left their house, Phil and Tammy exhorted him to tell Debby what was going on. He agreed to do so, but he didn't want anyone else to know.

When he got home, Debby could see that Tim had been crying. He said to her, "Debby, I'm not saved. Would you pray for me?"

Stunned, Debby said, "I can't pray for you. For 27 years you have been lying to me! I'm going for a walk."

Debby came back from her walk, but she was still upset. She went out again, and when she returned, she said, "Let's pray." They prayed together frequently from that time forward.

Phil and Tammy were leaving the next day on a ten-day trip. They visited with Tim one more time, and Phil told him to call Josh if he needed someone to talk to while they were away.

Tim felt strongly that God had given him Phil, Tammy, and Debby to help him spiritually. He didn't want to talk to anyone else, but he was in agony. Finally, one morning he called Josh and begged for prayer.

Josh told him there were a lot of people praying, but that they didn't know who it was they were praying for. "You didn't want people to know," Josh said. "Have you got a problem with pride, Tim? Why don't you want people to know?"

It was embarrassing. Tim was afraid of the judgmental attitudes of people who knew him. But that didn't matter anymore. He was desperate. He told Josh, "Put it in an email to everyone you know. 'Tim Van Hal needs salvation. Pray for him.'"

Tim then told his mother about his trouble. She wept painfully. He told her, "Mom, I'll never make another false profession again. Just pray for me."

Tim went to his church and told his pastor, "I'm not a Christian."

"What do you mean?" The pastor was completely flabbergasted. Tim was an upstanding community member. The pastor had never asked him about his salvation. It had just been assumed.

Tim asked to be put on the prayer chain for salvation. He then posted publicly on Facebook, "I'm not saved. I've been a fraud. If you're a person who prays, please pray for me."

The pastor got lots of calls from concerned community members who saw Tim's Facebook post. He decided against putting Tim's request on the prayer chain.

Many of Tim's acquaintances assumed that Tim had come under legalistic notions of salvation, and that the devil was attacking him with doubts. One came over to talk to him, intending to convince Tim that he was in error to question his salvation. Tim asked him, "Are you saved?"

"Yes."

"Are you sure?"

"Yes."

"I am that certain that I am not."

True Faith

After talking for a while, this friend suggested that Tim listen to a message on assurance of salvation. Debby wrote down the name of the sermon, *Biblical Tests of True Faith*, by Paul Washer on 1 John.

Overwhelmed and still feeling like his head was going to blow up from the pressure, Tim read Jeremiah 29:13, "And ye shall seek me, and find me, when ye shall search for me with all your heart."

Tim prayed, "Oh, God that is what I am going to do."

That night, after praying with Debby, Tim started to thank God for everything He had done in his life. He kept thinking of more and more things to be thankful for, and he named them all. By the time he was finished, his fear was gone. He thought to himself, "This is a good sign. I'm going to get saved. My fear of dying is gone."

A bit later, after listening a second time to Paul Washer's sermon on 1 John, Tim decided to call Phil. Instead of pouring out his woes as usual, he wanted to share something uplifting with Phil. He told him about the sermon.

Phil had already listened to the sermon. He told Tim, "I'm not here to pronounce whether anyone is saved or not, but that sermon doesn't have anything in it to encourage the lost." He then asked Tim why he didn't think he was saved.

"I don't understand things like you guys," Tim said.

Phil answered, "You'll be learning all your life. I've got a Dodge pick-up. It's fuel injected. I don't understand how it works. I turn the key, and it starts. It takes me where I want to go."

Tim realized that he had been saved the night that he had recognized God's goodness to him and had lifted up his heart in thanksgiving, October 17, 2020. He got baptized in November. Debby, still hurting from disillusion over having been lied to, nonetheless rejoiced in her husband's transformation. She was baptized, too. She had trusted in Christ for salvation as a teenager, but she hadn't received believer's baptism. As the couple was well-known in the community, the baptism was widely attended. Tim spoke boldly, glad to be free, not only of the fear of death, but also of the fear of man. He continues to use every opportunity to speak of the goodness of God and the forgiveness in Christ that is available to anyone who will seek Him.

These things have I written unto you that believe on the name of the Son of God; that ye may know that ye have eternal life.
—1 John 5:13

CHAPTER 20

Eternal Hope

The happy ending to Phil and Tammy's story is yet to come. Phil and Tammy have had a rewarding life on the earth, but their solid hope is in heaven. One day soon the true Prince will return to earth to take His bride to the Father's house. Phil and Tammy will go with Him. There will be no more sin and no more dying. No more sorrow, no more crying. No more misunderstanding and no more broken relationships. Only abundant life forevermore.

If they die before the church is raptured to heaven, Phil and Tammy will be with the Lord while they await reunification with their bodies which will be raised at the end of the age. Tammy has her funeral planned for those who may be left behind when she goes. She wants it to be a joyous event where cotton candy and Oreos are served.

Meanwhile, with at least five week-long camps planned for the summer, Phil and Tammy's schedule is full. Their winter is only slightly less busy. Whether selling wildlife engravings at art shows or driving taxi around town, Phil uses every opportunity to talk about the grace and goodness of his Lord Jesus. He and Tammy feel incredibly blessed to have been rooted in Valley City where they have many Christian friends and many opportunities for outreach with the gospel. They go to the senior center and the fitness center, and they have meals at the college cafeteria. They find hurting people everywhere, and the Lord opens doors for them to speak peace and hope into their lives.

One of the churches in town has a passion play at Easter time. Phil and Tammy take part in this, and they have found it to be a blessing to many, including their neighbor, Randy.

Randy Hoefs

For over sixty-five years, Randy thought he was living right, but he was thoroughly of the world. He had two small children when his first wife left him in the early eighties. Distraught and confused, he tried to grab at happiness, but his efforts only left him deeper in sin and misery. After a second failed relationship, a friend invited Randy to church. He felt the Lord tugging at his heart, but the world, the flesh, and the devil were tugging, too. Nonetheless, a seed was planted in his heart that later took root and grew.

The Lord granted mercies throughout the years, using both trial and blessing to draw Randy to Him. Randy had multiple surgeries on eyes, knee, and heart. In 2013, his second eye was affected with retinal detachment, and he had to retire from the post office.

After retirement, Randy worked at a restaurant and bar as a favor to a friend. He enjoyed the camaraderie there, but the presence of a bar had its pitfalls. Nonetheless, the Lord kept a hedge of protection around him. At the restaurant, Randy met Phil Kleymann and others who worked for ACB Construction. Randy sensed that these Christians had something that he wanted. Hungering for something, he quit work at the restaurant and started attending their church.

Phil invited Randy to the men's Bible study at the coffee house. There, the Word of God began to penetrate his heart. The clouds were parting, and bit by bit, Randy was leaving the sins of his former life behind.

On April 8, 2023, Randy attended the local passion play. He knew the story, but the enactment of the crucifixion made an impression on him like never before. When the Son of God went to the cross, Randy thought, "This shouldn't be. I'm the one who should be punished."

As he heard the loud whack of the hammer on the nails that pierced the Lord, the truth pierced his heart. It had to be this way! "He died for me!" It was as if the Lord said to him, "My Father and I love you." A cloak of peace wrapped around him. He now has a relationship with the Father because of the Son who died for him.

Because of his bad eyes, Randy can't see well enough to read much, but he listens to the Word of God. The Bible is alive to him, and he soaks it in. He talks about it with everyone who will let him.

Randy's confidence in God's goodness toward him cannot be shaken. He has had nightmares where Satan has tried to claim him. He saw himself on a fence with the Lord on the other side. The devil told him, "I own the fence. You're coming with me," but Randy boldly claimed the blood of Christ by which he is saved and brought in to the family of God. He is not on the fence anymore. He is crucified with Christ (Gal. 2:20).

> Cause me to hear thy lovingkindness in the morning; for in thee do I trust: cause me to know the way wherein I should walk; for I lift up my soul unto thee (Ps. 143:8).

Randy lives alone but loves to cook. Often, he will call the Kleymanns and have them pick him up for supper. He brings the meal to Phil and Tammy's or to Josh and Joanna's to share with them and Mick. Partaking of a meal together is the foretaste of the joys forevermore at the right hand of the Father.

Jail Ministry

Between camps and in the winter, Phil and Tammy, through their connection with the Gideons, participate in jail ministry. While speaking on a Sunday morning at the jail, Phil noticed a man in the back corner hanging on every word. After the study, others approached Phil and kept him from being able to go over and speak to Wade, but Tammy had seen him too. She sat down by him to talk. Wade was attentive and soaking in the truth she presented from the Bible. When the buzzer rang to leave, Phil stood in line behind Wade. He could hear the man talking to himself.

"What just hit me?" Wade said, shaking his head. "This is weird."

Three weeks later, Phil and Tammy saw Wade again. Tammy asked him, "What's your life been like the last few weeks?"

With a big grin, Wade said, "I have peace. I've never had peace before."

"Have you told these guys about it?" Tammy asked.

"No."

"Would you like to?"

"Yes." Wade testified to the group that Christ had changed him. Not long after, he was sent away to serve his sentence.

The transient nature of the jail community makes it difficult for preachers to see whether the fruit of their labor there is lasting. Though some men try to keep in touch, Phil and Tammy often don't know what happens to the guys after they leave.

Some of the men attending Sunday meetings asked if Phil and Tammy would be willing to come to the jail on Wednesdays as well. They wanted a Bible study with more in-depth teaching from the Word of God. Phil asked the lieutenant in charge and got permission to start Wednesday Bible studies, beginning in January, 2024.

One day in March, after the men had left, the lieutenant approached them. In an official tone, she said, "Can I have a word with you?"

"Sure," said Phil.

"Uh-oh," thought Tammy. "What did we do?"

As she spoke, the lieutenant's demeanor softened. She was warm and loving, but Tammy hardly noticed. She kept wondering what they had done wrong.

"These guys trust you," said the lieutenant. "Would you be willing to do one-on-one visits with them?"

"Absolutely!" What an answer to prayer! Phil and Tammy had been praying for ways to make a deeper impact on the guys than they had been able to do in a group setting.

One of the men was separated from the group because he was being bullied by the other guys. With tears in his eyes, this man said to Phil, "I hear we are getting together Wednesday. I really need it."

When they met with this man, he pulled a picture out of his Bible to show them. It was a drawing of the Maniac of Gadarenes that Phil had made and given to the prisoner after a Bible study. During the study, Phil had talked about the demon-filled Gadarene. He was uncontrollably wicked, but he was saved and subdued when he met Jesus.

"This is me," the man said, pointing at the picture. I don't want it to be. I want to be saved. I need the Lord."

As we all do.

Eternity

Those among us who are most blessed are those who see their need of a savior and are willing to be taken into the net of God's grace. The troubles of our present existence last only for a while. Eternal blessing awaits those who trust in Him.

"Righteousness, peace, joy in the Holy Spirit." This is the essence of the Kingdom of God. "He who serves Christ in these things is acceptable to God and approved by men" (Rom. 14:17-18 NKJV). As imperfect, broken vessels, Phil and Tammy's one desire is to obtain eternal life for themselves, those they love, and anyone willing to come along on the journey of faith. Fishing isn't a sport, an exercise, or a job to them. It is their life, and it comes naturally, taught to them by the Great Fisher of Men. They follow Him, and He honors their labors.

Thou wilt shew me the path of life: in thy presence is fulness of joy; at thy right hand there are pleasures for evermore.
—Psalm 16:11

AFTERWORD
Love, Joy, Peace

By Tammy Kleymann

As I walk this journey of opening up the rooms of my life, I've had to deal with several aha moments. As a survivor of physical abuse, there are new layers of healing still needed. I woke up this morning thinking about our Bible study at the jail this afternoon. We love the guys, and they love us. But when I go through three sets of locked doors to spend time around a table studying God's Word with them, I start panicking. When the guard locks the door behind me, I'm ten years old again, back in a room! I start feeling a burning in my gut, I start self-talking, telling myself to settle down. Sometimes it works, but not always. I have to ask the guard to let me out again to go to the bathroom. It's a long walk to the restroom. I'm digging my nails into my hands trying to distract myself from having to poo! Every part of me wants to say no to going to the jail. But I love these guys. I love spending time with them. They need to hear about God's love for them, Christ's love for them, His death for them.

Love

There are a few people in this world that I would give my life for. My husband, my kids, and my grandbabies. Mess with them and I could shred you up like a mother bear. When Josh was in his first year of high school, it was really hard for him. He hated the new public school he was attending. When I picked him up from school, he was so depressed. He had been in a private school all his life. Now he was hit with the kids and teachers using the Lord's name in vain. One Friday he had a football game. He didn't get to eat lunch that day, because he was out of money in his lunch bank. I had an extra hamburger with me when I got to the game. I saw him from a distance, and he motioned to me that he was starving, so I ran down to the fence and tossed him the burger. His coach got so mad at him and was cussing him out. The next Monday Josh didn't want to go to school—whether it be he was so embarrassed by me or he hated all the cussing he heard all the time. I made him get out of the car and go to school. When I picked him up that afternoon, he was super upset. He wanted to drop out of school. I was so mad I jumped out of the car stormed into the boy's locker room, yelling for the coach. I let that coach have it. I yelled at him. In fact, I took on the whole coaching staff while the entire team stood there as I lined them out. I told them that they will never speak to my kid that way again. I said, "I don't cuss at him, and you won't either!" The head coach sat in his chair giggling at me, not ridiculing me, but agreeing with me. The coach I was yelling at started apologizing to me and told me he would let Josh be a starter at the next game. I told him, "I could care a less about your stupid football team. I am trying to keep my kid in school, and you cussing him out all the time isn't helping!" Josh was never cussed at again.

 I'll stand in front of a semi-truck if I have to for those I love. That's what the Lord did for us. That is love! I own that same love, it motivates me, it lives in me, it drives me. That kind of love motivates me to forgive. The same love that helps me forgive also covers a multitude of sins. I've had to forgive a lot. Today there's a new battle, and I have to lay hold of that same love to deal with it.

Joy

Despite the first eighteen years, I've had an abundant life. God has been so good to Phil and me. There were times in the middle of a birthday party, hearing the kids laughing and playing, that I sat there and enjoyed the moment, making a mental note of the moment. I thanked the Lord for the life He enabled me to give my family. It's not perfect. Rather, it is full of mistakes. I've tried to apply my life verse of esteeming others higher than myself. Giving, loving, working, sacrificing, speaking truth even when it means sacrificing a relationship. I'll side with my Heavenly Father every time.

Staying in God's will is always the best place to be. There's beauty in the ashes. We just abide, and the beauty appears. It's miraculous. God uses my ashes to reach children who have been victimized. What beauty! I forgave all my parents, and we had a beautiful ending. I'm here to tell you the joy is real!

Peace

The opposite of peace is chaos. Life is chaotic. The first eighteen years of my life was absolute chaos. It's been difficult going back in time and compiling all of this! The good news is that the Good News of Jesus Christ brings peace! I wanted my story written to tell my readers to embrace your past but realize that you are able to change your future. I fought to provide peace in my home. I fought hard to keep peace within me. The only way possible is with the help of the Holy Spirit, the third person of the Trinity, and God's precious Word. It's living and powerful. It transforms the mind. I battle the thoughts in my mind, as we all do. Being in His Word sanctifies my mind and fuels the peace. I'm eternally and daily grateful for my Bible. It needs to be rebound, and I almost have an anxiety attack just thinking about being separated from it. I know how much I need it. It keeps me at perfect peace! Another tool God has given me is prayer. I like to pray out loud. I sort out a lot of chaos in prayer. The Lord wakes me up at night with burdens that only He can bear. Taking those burdens to Him calms the chaos in me.

There will be another aha moment that will rear its ugly head. That's the life of a victim. We have unexpected PTSD attacks from living life. These will demand more spiritual grit. Getting old, living life, things come up. I'll have to face my own death or the death of a loved one — if we don't go in the rapture! In all of life there's the joy of loving and serving my Savior that blesses us. I plan on staying active for Him till the very end! People can come and go, but my God will never leave me nor forsake me.

Love, Joy, Peace. *The greatest is Love.*

Let nothing be done through selfish ambition or conceit, but in lowliness of mind let each esteem others better than himself. Let each of you look out not only for his own interests, but also for the interests of others. —Philippians 2:3-4 NKJV

Scripture Index

Genesis 4:7 86	Romans 8:6 24
2 Samuel 12:23 94	Romans 12:17-21 62-3
Psalm 16:11 172	Romans 12:19 77
Psalm 37:4 41	Romans 14:17-18 171
Psalm 40:2-3 156	1 Corinthians 10:13 72
Psalm 103:12 117	1 Corinthians 10:21 127
Psalm 118:8-9 16	2 Corinthians 5:17 46
Psalm 130:7 68	2 Corinthians 12:9 79
Psalm 143:8 169	Galations 2:20 169
Proverbs 11:30 35	Ephesians 2:8-9 .... 5, 116
Proverbs 18:16 90	Ephesians 4:32 73
Isaiah 65:24 90	Ephesians 6:2-3 66
Jeremiah 29:13 165	Philippians 1:6 77
Lamentations 3:22 73	Philippians 2:3-4 176
Daniel 3 108	Philippians 2:12 95
Micah 5:2 115	Philippians 4:6-7 87
Matthew 4:19 118	1 Thessalonians 3:9 137
Matthew 4:20 150	2 Thessalonians 1:7-8 73
Matthew 7:7 .... 30, 143	2 Timothy 4:5 113
Matthew 10:30 39	Hebrews 9:27 37
Matthew 28:20 96	Hebrews 11:13 53
Luke 7:50 156	Hebrews 13:5 61
Luke 15:7 48	James 3:8 144
Luke 15:11-32 142	James 5:16 41
John 3:3 46	1 Peter 2:11 159
John 3:16 32, 109, 125, 130	1 Peter 2:24 .... 52, 117
John 10:7-9 132	1 John 165
John 10:11-15 .... 98, 133	1 John 5:4 104
John 14:1-6 122	1 John 5:9-13 115-6
John 20:29 47-48	1 John 5:13. 123-4, 136, 166
Romans 1:28-32 130	Revelation 2:5 151

[1] Seamands, David A. *Healing of Memories*, Wheaton Illinois: Victor Books, 1985.
[2] Kim Phuc Phan Thi, *Fire Road: A Memoir of Hope*, Tyndale Momentum, 2017, p.265.
[3] https://overcomersinchrist.org/
[4] An elder in the church and Mary Fear's son-in-law, husband of Marion, *see p. 39*.
[5] *For Joanna's story see,* Nita Brainard: *Box T and the Choices That Made It God's Ranch*, pp. 105-8, available on Amazon.

Made in the USA
Monee, IL
12 June 2024